Comments on other *Amazing Stories* from readers & reviewers

"*Tightly written volumes filled with lots of wit and humour about famous and infamous Canadians.*"
Eric Shackleton, *The Globe and Mail*

"*The heightened sense of drama and intrigue, combined with a good dose of human interest is what sets* Amazing Stories *apart.*"
Pamela Klaffke, *Calgary Herald*

"*This is popular history as it should be... For this price, buy two and give one to a friend.*"
Terry Cook, a reader from Ottawa, on **Rebel Women**

"*Glasner creates the moment of the explosion itself in graphic detail...she builds detail upon gruesome detail to create a convincingly authentic picture.*"
Peggy McKinnon, *The Sunday Herald*, on **The Halifax Explosion**

"*It was wonderful...I found I could not put it down. I was sorry when it was completed.*"
Dorothy F. from Manitoba on **Marie-Anne Lagimodière**

"*Stories are rich in description, and bristle with a clever, stylish realness.*"
Mark Weber, *Central Alberta Advisor*, on **Ghost Town Stories II**

"*A compelling read. Bertin...has selected only the most intriguing tales, which she narrates with a wealth of detail.*"
Joyce Glasner, *New Brunswick Reader*, on **Strange Events**

"*The resulting book is one readers will want to share with all the women in their lives.*"
Lynn Martel, *Rocky Mountain Outlook*, on **Women Explorers**

CALGARY FLAMES

CALGARY FLAMES

Fire on Ice

HOCKEY

by Monte Stewart

PUBLISHED BY ALTITUDE PUBLISHING CANADA LTD.
1500 Railway Avenue, Canmore, Alberta T1W 1P6
www.altitudepublishing.com
1-800-957-6888

Extreme care has been taken to ensure that all information presented in
this book is accurate and up to date. Neither the author nor the
publisher can be held responsible for any errors.

Publisher   Stephen Hutchings
Associate Publisher   Kara Turner
Editors   Stephen Smith, Joan Dixon

We acknowledge the financial support of the Government
of Canada through the Book Publishing Industry Development
Program (BPIDP) for our publishing activities.

Altitude GreenTree Program
Altitude Publishing will plant twice as many trees as were used
in the manufacturing of this product.

We acknowledge the support of the Canada Council for the Arts which
in 2003 invested $21.7 million in writing and publishing throughout Canada.

Canada Council   Conseil des Arts
for the Arts   du Canada

National Library of Canada Cataloguing in Publication Data

Stewart, Monte, 1962-
Calgary Flames / Monte Stewart.

(Amazing stories)
Includes bibliographical references.
ISBN 1-55153-794-X

1. Calgary Flames (Hockey team)--History.
I. Title. II. Series: Amazing stories (Canmore, Alta.)

GV848.C28S74 2004   796.962'64'09712338   C2004-903745-5

An application for the trademark for Amazing Stories™
has been made and the registered trademark is pending.

Printed and bound in Canada by Friesens
2 4 6 8 9 7 5 3

In memory of Ed Whalen

Contents

Prologue

March 9, 1991: Calgary Flames vs. St. Louis Blues
It was supposed to be just another regular season game, but he made it one to remember.

According to the scouts, he was too small to play in the National Hockey League. The Flames had only drafted him — in the eighth round in 1987 — because their Salt Lake City farm club needed someone who could help boost sagging attendance. Calgary's general manager at the time, Cliff Fletcher, thought the fans would love his determination, his speed, and his feisty play. The GM was right.

But the kid from Manitoba surprised almost everyone by making the Flames. Fletcher was so impressed with his progress that he gave up Brett Hull to the Blues. The Golden Brett had become a superstar there and given St. Louis one of the most potent power plays in the league.

Tonight, it was the job of "the Littlest Flame," as he was known, to stop Hull when Calgary was killing penalties. But he didn't just stop Hull, he commandeered the puck and scored a shorthanded goal. And then another. And then another. He scored three shorthanded goals as Calgary doubled the Blues 8-4. No other Flame — no other player in the NHL — had ever done that.

Calgary Flames

And Theoren Fleury is only one of the amazing parts of the story of the Calgary Flames.

Chapter 1
A New Home in Calgary

Nothing like this had ever happened when Cliff Fletcher was with Montreal. Rising up through the ranks of the Canadiens organization as a scout and executive, he didn't have to worry about how big the crowds were, or who would pay the bills. Tickets to a National Hockey League game at the Forum were as precious as a Rembrandt. Heck, some people might have sold one of the Old Masters' paintings just to see the likes of Jean Beliveau, Yvan Cournoyer, Guy Lafleur, and a young goaltender named Ken Dryden.

But Fletcher, the Flames general manager, was discovering that Atlanta, in the late 1970s, was definitely not like Montreal. Still, he strove to make the Atlanta franchise like the Canadiens, just as he had with the St. Louis Blues, where he trained as a chief scout and assistant general manager before he was hired as the Atlanta Flames' first general manager in the summer of 1972.

Baseball was the big game in Atlanta, thanks to Braves slugger Hank Aaron, who had broken Babe Ruth's all-time home run record. Football and basketball — pro or college, it didn't matter — were also very popular. Hockey was just an afterthought.

The Flames had been in the NHL since 1972-73, when they joined the league at the same time as the New York Islanders. But the crowds were small, the club was struggling, and the owners (a group of Georgia businessmen headed by real estate developer Tom Cousins) were tired of losing money. Unlike Major League Baseball, the National Football League, or the National Basketball Association, the NHL did not have the luxury of millions of dollars worth of television revenue. There was only one way for the club to turn its fortunes around. It would have to sell more tickets.

Fletcher could not count on a rivalry with an opposing team to bring people through the turnstiles. The Flames did not have any nearby opponents in the southwestern U.S. sunbelt. The Islanders were their biggest rivals, but they were way up in New York. The team had to do something else, or get someone else, who would put people in the seats.

The GM decided it was time to take action. He needed to make a move that would generate buzz. In coming years, he would receive the nickname "Trader Cliff" because of his fondness for making big deals. Some reporters believed there was no trade that he didn't like.

Most of the NHL's stars at that time hailed from Canada, which produced more NHLers than any other country. The trouble was, most Atlanta hockey fans did not know much about Canada. Like many southerners, they thought it was under snow 12 months of the year. As good as the player might be, a Canadian hockey star might still not appeal to average Americans. European players, like Swedes Borje Salming and Inge Hammerstrom of the Toronto Maple Leafs, were just starting to enter the league. But they would also be a tough sell in the hometown of Coca Cola. Fletcher decided instead to stake the fate of the Atlanta Flames franchise on an all-American hero.

Few people were familiar with the name Jim Craig before the 1980 Winter Olympics. Now, it seemed, almost everyone in America knew him. A college player from Easton, Massachusetts, he had made the U.S. Olympic team — a squad comprised mostly of college players like himself — under coach Herb Brooks. Craig then backstopped the underdog U.S. to the gold medal in Lake Placid by upsetting the favoured Soviet Union.

Their triumph became known as the Miracle On Ice. In a year when America was struggling to deal with the hostage-taking in Iran and another oil crisis, the gold medal victory was a real treat. Craig was lauded as an American hero. His heroics helped spur a rise in hockey's popularity in the U.S. Eventually, the U.S. would become a perennial contender for Olympic, world championship, and World Cup gold. The American victory would also inspire a generation of youngsters to dream of becoming professional hockey players just like Jim Craig.

Fletcher believed that Craig, whom the Flames had drafted in the fourth round in 1977, would be the perfect fit for the struggling team. He signed him to a contract and Craig came out for his first game as a Flame draped in an American flag. Craig's signing would also set the stage for the game's internationalization as Fletcher and other general managers started to look beyond North America for talent. The Flames' expectations of Craig were enormous. Contrary to his Olympic experience, he was expected to win and save a franchise.

Craig joined Atlanta just six days after his stunning gold medal performance. His debut produced a rare sellout at The Omni as he stopped 24 of 25 shots to lead the Flames to a 4-1 win over the Colorado Rockies.

Unfortunately, Craig could not continue his magic. He went winless in three more regular season starts. In the playoffs that year, the New York Rangers quickly extinguished the Flames in four games. As it turned out, America's hero would last only part of one season with the Flames — which was their last in Atlanta.

At the end of the 1979-80 campaign, after not finding the solution to his team's woes within the U.S., Fletcher decided to look outside the country. He turned his attention north to Canada where, following the merger of the NHL and the World Hockey Association (WHA), the game was enjoying a boom. That season, the NHL had welcomed the Winnipeg Jets, Quebec Nordiques, Hartford Whalers, and Edmonton Oilers. Edmonton was fortunate to feature the young superstar Wayne Gretzky.

Edmonton's southerly rival, Calgary, was home to Canada's oil and gas industry and fearless entrepreneurs who liked to work hard and play hard. Calgary pined for an NHL club of its own too, especially after its misadventures with the WHA.

The Calgary Broncos were actually supposed to be one of the WHA's original 10 clubs in 1972. But the Broncos never played a game because owner Bob Brownridge suddenly became ill and didn't pay the $100,000 franchise fee. Three years later, Calgary got another chance to become home to a WHA club. Vancouver businessman Jim Pattison moved the Blazers to Calgary from the west coast and changed the team's name to the Cowboys, in keeping with the city's long association with the Calgary Stampede, the world's richest rodeo. During the Cowboys' two seasons, they were known more for their colourful characters than their on-ice success. Many fans thought goaltender Don "Smokey" McLeod was crazy. He was the only player in pro hockey who used a curved stick to help him shoot the puck out of his team's zone. He also used a first baseman's glove because he could handle the puck better with it. Cowboy forward Rick Jodzio helped maintain the WHA's reputation as a fighters' league. In the first round of the playoffs in their first year, and the only year they made the playoffs, Jodzio jumped Quebec Nordiques superstar defenceman Marc Tardif, prompting one of the largest bench-clearing brawls in pro-hockey history. Tardif suffered brain injuries and lost several teeth. Jodzio pleaded guilty to an assault charge, was fined and suspended. After their second season, the Cowboys folded with the rest of the WHA and were not among the teams that merged into the NHL.

Calgary fans were shocked at the idea that their city could not support a professional hockey franchise. Cowtown had in fact enjoyed a rich hockey history since Alberta became a province in 1905. Calgary's memorable teams included the Calgary Mustangs during World War II, the Calgary Stampeders senior club of the 1960s and 1970s, and the Calgary Centennials of the Western Canada Junior Hockey League in the early 1970s. The Centennials featured a tall lanky goaltender named John Davidson, now a well-known hockey broadcaster. They were coached by the legendary Scotty Munro, whose name graces the league championship trophy. During his half-century in hockey, cigar-chomping Munro had tutored several future NHLers: hall-of-famers Bert Olmstead and Glenn Hall, and Calgary native Mike Rogers, another broadcaster.

A New Home in Calgary

While the Flames were struggling in Atlanta, both on the ice and financially, six ambitious oilmen were quietly inquiring about bringing an NHL club to Calgary. The oilmen, including a geologist named Harley Hotchkiss, and a couple of brothers, Doc and Byron (B.J.) Seaman, wanted to do something to help build their community and help amateur hockey. They believed that an NHL franchise could do just that. The group quietly approached the Alberta government about funding a state-of-the-art rink because many people believed that the WHA Cowboys had struggled because they played in the old Calgary Corral. Thanks to a young mayor named Ralph Klein, the city was already putting together a bid to host the 1988 Winter Olympics. The plans called for a new arena. Hotchkiss and the Seamans promised to use the club's proceeds to help fund amateur hockey in the province.

Confident that they could get the money for the arena, the Hotchkiss group offered to purchase the Atlanta Flames from Cousins and his partners for US$14 million. The Cousins real estate consortium wanted to sell the club because land prices had fallen.

But Vancouver real estate tycoon Nelson Skalbania had got wind of the Calgarians' plans. The rogue was notorious for flipping properties, including sports franchises. A few years earlier, as the owner of the WHA Indianapolis Racers, he had sold the playing rights of teenage phenom Wayne Gretzky to Edmonton Oilers' owner Peter Pocklington. Different accounts of the trade had the two owners working out the deal either on a napkin in a restaurant, or over a game of backgammon.

Skalbania snatched the Flames from the willing Atlanta owners, outbidding the Calgary group by a couple of million. He announced that the team would be moving to Calgary. A week after buying the Flames, Skalbania approached the six oilmen and offered them a stake in the franchise. They bought in and eventually took over the franchise from Skalbania, who by then was on the verge of personal bankruptcy — due to other impulsive deals.

So, on May 21, 1980, the Atlanta Flames became the Calgary Flames and Calgary's flaming 'C' logo replaced Atlanta's flaming 'A'. Fletcher moved north with the team and resumed his duties as general manager. However, Jim Craig, the would-be saviour of the Atlanta team, was dealt to the Boston Bruins for draft picks. He spent only part of one season with Boston then was shipped to the minors and the U.S. national program. He did not get another chance with an NHL club until he signed a free-agent contract with Minnesota in 1983-84. He played only three games with the North Stars and wound down his career in the minors with Salt Lake. Just four years after guiding the U.S. to Olympic glory, Jim Craig's pro hockey career was over.

But after a rocky start in Atlanta, the Flames' best years were about to begin.

Chapter 2
Loyal Al and Badger Bob

Al MacNeil became the first coach in Calgary Flames history. He would become the club's longest-serving employee — over a quarter century.

MacNeil first broke into the NHL in the 1950s — a time when few players from his home province of Nova Scotia reached the six-team National Hockey League. Nova Scotia players faced an uphill struggle because there was no major junior league in the Maritimes. With no draft yet in place, NHL clubs protected players from teams in their areas, regardless of where the player was born and raised. The Toronto Maple Leafs, under legendary Conn Smythe, had been given more leeway than other clubs so controlled much of Eastern

Canada. It was quite a coup for a kid from Nova Scotia to get to play for the Toronto Marlboros in the Leafs feeder system. MacNeil earned his crack at the NHL captaining the Toronto Marlboros to the 1955-56 Memorial Cup championship.

Generously listed at 5-foot-10, MacNeil was a short, stocky defenceman in an era when, like today, teams looked for large rear guards. Despite shuffling between the minors and the NHL, he managed to play 524 games over his 15-year career with Toronto, Montreal, Chicago, New York, and the expansion Pittsburgh. As the end of his playing days approached, he became a player-coach. At the start of the 1970-71 season, MacNeil finally retired as a player and devoted his full attention to coaching as an assistant with the Montreal Canadiens. He dreamed of one day becoming a head coach in the NHL.

His chance would come sooner than he, or anyone else, imagined. In 1970, the Canadiens had missed the post-season for the first time since 1948 — an unforgivable calamity in Montreal. Just 23 games into the next regular season, the struggling Canadiens fired coach Claude Ruel. Their general manager Sam Pollock appointed MacNeil to replace Ruel. Despite having no NHL head coaching experience, MacNeil was expected to lead the hallowed Habs back to the playoffs.

As if those expectations were not enough, MacNeil faced additional pressure off the ice. He took the Habs' reins during the most tumultuous time in Quebec's modern history.

Quebec's separatist sentiments had erupted in an

episode of terrorism. On October 16, 1970, for the first time in Canadian history outside of war, Prime Minister Pierre Trudeau invoked the War Measures Act. An extremist group known as the Front de Libération du Québec (FLQ) had kidnapped British diplomat James Cross and Quebec Labour Minister Pierre Laporte, who was later found dead in the trunk of a car. The War Measures Act suspended the Canadian Bill of Rights, and gave the federal government sweeping powers to search and arrest people connected with the FLQ. Army tanks rolled through downtown Montreal. The events left a deep sense of distrust between anglophones and francophones — which extended right into the Canadiens' dressing room. MacNeil, an anglophone from the Maritimes who did not speak French, had inadvertently walked into the middle of the October Crisis. He replaced Ruel only a day after Cross was released.

Despite becoming a beacon of political discontent, MacNeil did guide the Habs back to the playoffs. He took the team all the way to the Stanley Cup finals, when he dared to bench Henri Richard, one of the most popular players in the Habs' history. Richard had called MacNeil the worst coach for whom he had ever played and the controversy intensified the bitter French–English relations prevalent across the province. The Montreal Forum was the subject of numerous bomb threats. MacNeil and his family were placed under police protection. But after losing the first two games of the final in Chicago, the Canadiens came back to win the

Cup — on two goals by Richard. Richard's success spelled MacNeil's demise.

The first Nova Scotia-born Stanley Cup-champion coach also became the first Stanley Cup-champion coach to lose his job following that season. MacNeil said he resigned. Members of Canadiens' management implied that he was fired. Nonetheless, still loyal to the organization, MacNeil became coach and general manager of its farm team, the Nova Scotia Voyageurs. He led the Voyageurs to three Calder Cup championships and was twice named the American Hockey League coach of the year. Even though he was then only a minor-league coach, MacNeil was named as an assistant coach of Team Canada's squad of NHLers for both the 1971 and 1976 Canada Cup tournaments. No other minor-league coach had accomplished that feat.

But MacNeil longed for a chance to return to the NHL. Fletcher and MacNeil had been old friends since their days together with the Montreal organization. When Fletcher offered MacNeil the Atlanta Flames' coaching post in 1978-79, MacNeil jumped at the chance. Despite the turmoil surrounding the team's future, MacNeil put the Flames in the playoffs.

When the Flames moved to Calgary, they instantly became the most popular team in town. They even dethroned the Canadian Football League's beloved Stampeders. But unlike his days in Montreal, MacNeil did not have a bunch of stars at his disposal to work with. However, he did have one player who was clearly more offensively gifted than the rest — Kent Nilsson.

Nilsson, who had toiled under MacNeil in Atlanta, would become the first of many unlikely Calgary Flames heroes. The team drafted him in the fourth round in 1976, when he appeared to be a long shot to make the NHL. The league at the time featured only a handful of Europeans. Instead of joining the Flames right away, he stayed in his native Sweden for one more season and then signed with the WHA Winnipeg Jets. Ironically, Nilsson posted 107 points in each of those two seasons. When the Jets joined the NHL, the Atlanta Flames were able to re-claim him under the terms of the merger.

In his first season in Calgary, Nilsson earned the nickname "Magic Man" because of his deft passing, creative stick-handling, and ability to score consistently — with apparently little effort. He led the Flames with 49 goals and 82 assists and finished third in league scoring behind Wayne Gretzky and Marcel Dionne. In the process, he became the first European-trained player to produce more than 100 points in a single NHL season.

Thanks to Nilsson and hard-working players like veteran centre Don Lever and rookie winger Jim Peplinski, the Calgary Flames finished third in their division. They advanced all the way to the Stanley Cup semi-finals against the upstart Minnesota North Stars. Alas, the slipper did not fit the Cinderella team and the North Stars ousted the

Flames in six games.

The following season, the Flames could not match their first year's success, however Fletcher swung a deal that would help the franchise become a Stanley Cup contender for many years to come. On November 25, 1981, Flames GM "Trader" Cliff acquired Lanny McDonald from Colorado.

McDonald, known even then by his trademark bushy moustache, gave the Flames instant credibility as a team to be reckoned with. His middle name — King — would soon symbolize his status with the Flames.

Although McDonald had grown up on a farm near Hanna, Alberta, he had thrived in Toronto. Drafted fourth overall in 1973, he had become one of the Maple Leafs' dominant players, along with his buddy, linemate and captain, Darryl Sittler. They turned the Leafs back into a legitimate Stanley Cup contender under cantankerous owner Harold Ballard. But McDonald had been caught in the middle of a feud between Ballard, general manager Punch Imlach, and Sittler. McDonald was traded to Colorado as a way to get back at Sittler, who had a no-trade clause in his contract.

Even today, Toronto fans, players, and unusually sentimental reporters grow sad while recalling McDonald's trade. Many years later, they can still recall where they were and what they were doing when they heard their beloved Lanny had been traded. McDonald enjoyed his brief stint in Colorado, under colourful Rockies coach Don Cherry, but the financially struggling franchise was a cellar dweller.

Therefore, in addition to helping the Flames franchise, the trade to Calgary boosted McDonald's briefly stalled career. As he had been with the Toronto Maple Leafs, he became the inspirational leader for the Flames.

In spite of Lanny, Calgary was swept 3-0 in the first round of the 1982 playoffs by the Vancouver Canucks. Featuring former Toronto coach Roger Neilson and McDonald's old pal Tiger Williams, the Canucks later qualified for the Stanley Cup finals for the first time in the franchise's history. At the end of the season, GM Fletcher decided that a coaching change was necessary and fired his friend Al MacNeil. As he had done with Montreal, the former coach remained loyal to the Flames and accepted a management post.

Fletcher found his new coach in an unlikely place. "Badger" Bob Johnson earned his nickname by coaching for 15 seasons at the University of Wisconsin, where he won three National Collegiate Athletic Association hockey titles. While at Wisconsin, Johnson also coached U.S. national teams and the 1976 Olympic team. But the Minneapolis, Minnesota, native had no previous professional experience, either as a player or coach. Many observers wondered how he would handle the brash pros, who were used to playing for ex-NHLers. Although they might not say so publicly, it's widely acknowledged that NHLers prefer to play for coaches who have also played in the league.

Johnson, perhaps because he served as a U.S. Army medic during the Korean War, was not fazed by what others thought about him. His positive attitude, his obvious love for the game, and his genuine concern for people were remarkable. "Some people looked at him and shook their heads, as if he were the Nutty Professor," wrote hockey reporter George Johnson. "He certainly didn't lack for ego or confidence, but there was an ingratiating naivete about his enthusiasm that couldn't help but win you over. He had time for anyone interested in hockey."

Another reporter covering the Flames, Eric Duhatschek, recalled a road trip to Toronto when Bob Johnson's character shone through loud and clear. Johnson and many of the Flames players who were originally from Toronto or other parts of Ontario were eating breakfast with family in the café of the hotel where the team was staying. Badger Bob got up from his table, popped around the restaurant and assured the players' parents that the team was looking after their boys. Duhatschek, a Toronto native, also happened to be dining there with his mother and father. "Don't worry, Mr. and Mrs. Duhatschek, we're taking good care of Eric, too," said Johnson.

Coaches traditionally were not supposed to get along with reporters. Badger was not afraid to be different — in many ways. Rather than kick garbage cans or yell at his players after a loss, as many other coaches would have done, Johnson looked for the positives of any performance, no matter how lopsided the score. He also lived by his favourite expression — "It's a great day for hockey!" — and displayed quirky mannerisms behind the bench. During games, he frequently tugged on his large nose, yanked on his eyebrows, or scribbled his observations on a small notepad. At that time, no other NHL coach took notes during games. Today, because of Johnson, it is hard to find one who does not.

The American-born coach also opened the NHL's eyes to players from his homeland, who despite the 1980 Miracle On Ice, were still often ignored on draft day. "Badger paved the way for Americans to play at [the NHL] level," said American defenceman Gary Suter, who played under him for two seasons in Calgary. "Before guys like him, hockey was a Canadians-only game. People like him had a lot to do with guys like me making it to the NHL. We owe him a lot."

Because of his willingness to employ unusual coaching methods, his attention to detail, and his competitive nature, Johnson managed to get the most out of his players —regardless of where they came from. In 1982-83, Johnson extracted the best results from his superstars — Nilsson and McDonald. Picking up where he had left off the previous season, McDonald tallied 66 goals — more than any Flames player, in Calgary or Atlanta, had ever scored before. Nilsson faced high expectations because of his previous offensive numbers and his obvious brilliance with the puck. He led the team in overall scoring with 104 points, to add to McDonald's 98. As a result of the two stars' exploits, the Flames placed second in the Smythe Division behind their arch rivals, the Edmonton Oilers.

Calgary Flames

In the post-season, the Flames avenged their previous year's loss to the Canucks by eliminating Vancouver in four games. The Flames, however, were no match for Gretzky, Mark Messier, and company. The Oilers, a predominantly young team, won the best-of-seven Smythe Division finals in five games. It was the first of many great Calgary–Edmonton playoff series to come.

McDonald was named to the NHL's second all-star team and received the Bill Masterton Trophy for sportsmanship, perseverance, and dedication to hockey. He would have preferred to hoist another trophy — the Stanley Cup.

Chapter 3
Unsung Heroes

It was January 1985. Lanny McDonald was starting to wonder whether he would ever get a chance to win the Stanley Cup. He knew that first the Flames would have to beat Edmonton in the playoffs — which they had never done before. After bowing to the Oilers in the 1982-83 playoffs, Calgary had lost to them again — in seven games — in the second round of the following year's post-season. The Oilers went on to claim their first ever Stanley Cup. The message was clear. If the Flames could beat Edmonton, they could contend for the Cup. But in 1984-85, Winnipeg upset the Flames, denying them a rematch with the Oilers, who captured their second straight Stanley Cup. Now midway through the 1985-86 regular season, it looked like Calgary would have a hard time just making the playoffs. The Flames had just suffered their eighth straight loss — against Edmonton.

"Watching the Calgary Flames right now is like watching a pickup game on a pond," said Fletcher. "The effort has been there, but our defence had better get back to the basics." But Badger Bob was more positive than ever. "Yeah, 51 shots on the Oilers, sounds like a pretty good pickup game to me," he retorted.

The loss to Edmonton had been entertaining for another reason. During one altercation, Oilers tough guy Marty McSorley's sweater came off and centre Doug Risebrough snatched it. Sitting in the penalty box, much to the delight of fans, Risebrough shredded McSorley's jersey with his skates. After the game, the Oilers hung McSorley's tattered jersey in their dressing room for the media to see. Edmonton general manager Glen Sather, a former Montreal Canadien, announced that his friendship with Risebrough, also a former Canadien, was over. He vowed to send the Flames a bill for $1,000, although nobody was sure how he came up with that figure.

"Fletcher's so paranoid about our team," said Sather. "He thinks the only way the Flames can beat us is by beating the crap out of us, which is ridiculous." The win actually marked Edmonton's 17th win over the Flames in their last 20 meetings. But at that time, the Flames had been losing to everyone.

Unsung Heroes

Coach Johnson could not explain the team's funk. For the first time in his lengthy career, he did not have an answer for his questioners. "You go to pick up the dry cleaning and they ask you what's wrong with your club, you go to buy a paper and they want to know what's wrong, and you buy gas and the guy wants to know what's wrong," he said. "I can't tell anyone how to solve it, because this has never happened to me before. I can't look back and say what I did in '62 because it just didn't happen. I've always been fortunate to have winners."

The successful coach refused to give up hope. Instead, he decided to get creative on and off the ice. Doing his impression of a batter in baseball, Johnson swung an imaginary bat and told the team that they should not think too much. To help his players relax, he handed out a yoga assignment. He also became more cheerful than ever. Good game, he would say after another loss. Good job, he would say, to a disheartened player, praising him for a goal or a check. Although it did not affect anything in the standings, the positive attitude became an absolute psychological necessary for Johnson and his team. "You need PMA (positive mental attitude)... and all you can do is look in the mirror and come out all fired up," he counselled.

Between December 14 and January 7, the Flames continued to suffer. Eleven straight losses, no ties. The most humiliating moment came when the Flames lost 9-1 at home to Hartford. But Johnson advised his players and reporters not to worry, because the Flames had the other teams exactly where they wanted them. Other clubs would now take the Flames lightly, leaving themselves vulnerable. Reporters and players just shook their heads at the unusual coach.

Amazingly, the coach's words would prove prophetic. The Flames ended the losing streak with a 5-4 overtime victory at home against Vancouver — the same team that had started them on their nosedive. Over the rest of the regular season, Calgary would never again lose two games in a row — thanks to one special newcomer.

On February 1, 1986, Trader Cliff acquired Joey Mullen from the St. Louis Blues. Mullen was a player who knew the meaning of adversity. Always considered small for a hockey player, Mullen grew up in the notorious Hell's Kitchen neighbourhood of New York City. Prostitutes and drug dealers frequented the area, and violence was a way of life, but Joey and his brothers concentrated on sports instead. Their father happened to be the guy who drove the Zamboni between periods of Rangers games at Madison Square Garden. Both Joey and his brother Brian made it to the NHL after learning the game playing roller hockey with a ball of black tape.

Although Mullen excelled with a couple of New York City junior teams, he was not offered a university scholarship, which was then the ticket to the NHL for most American players. So he scraped together $700 to cover his first year at Boston College before earning a scholarship his second year. Mullen averaged better than two points per game during both seasons at BC, but no NHL team chose to draft him.

Someone from the Blues finally noticed him and the club signed him as a free agent. In each of his four-plus seasons with St. Louis, he notched at least a point per game. He was also a consistent playoff performer, although just before he was traded, he had been held pointless in the 1984-85 post-season. Minnesota swept the Blues in three games.

Looking back, Mullen's trade for three journeymen was inexplicable and, undoubtedly, one that St. Louis general manager Ron Caron would regret. The Missouri city's loss was Calgary's gain. As soon as he arrived in Calgary, Mullen started scoring and again produced better than a point per game. He was also a gentleman on the ice, receiving only 11 penalty minutes.

Mullen was just one of many unsung heroes on the Flames roster that season. Like him, they knew all about hardship and some of them were not expected to make the NHL. Winger Colin Patterson had excelled at Canada's other sport — lacrosse — and as a teenager helped the national team to a world championship bronze medal. But he had not been considered much of a prospect at hockey. After playing tier II junior in Ontario, Patterson headed to Clarkson College, a small school in New York. He was intent on getting a degree in business and marketing while playing hockey on the side. Never drafted, he never expected to play in the NHL because as he said, "to be honest, I wasn't that good."

A Flames scout spotted Patterson on a visit to Clarkson to watch one of Patterson's teammates, Jim Laing. Laing, ironically, was drafted by the Flames but never played a game with Calgary. Calgary offered Patterson a free agent contract. He jumped at the chance to play pro, even though he expected to toil in the minors. His father, an engineer, and his mother, a teacher, both valued education more highly, and were not very happy with their son's decision to leave college early. "And they felt, much like I sort of felt at the time, too, was I really going to play in the NHL? But at the time, you know, the money that they were offering ($30,000) for the minor-league salary was very good. I wasn't going to make that anywhere else. I said: 'Well, if I can play four years in the minors, that way I'd be able to make some money and start a career afterwards.' "

Patterson would eventually get his marketing and management degree from Clarkson and become a successful executive with Shaw TV. But he would only play 13 games in the minors while becoming a mainstay with the Flames. Playing every shift like it was his last, he delighted Johnson with his hard-working ways. "He said I was a project for him, he was going to make me better — and he did," recalled Patterson.

While Patterson was becoming a better defensive player, Hakan Loob was displaying offensive prowess in his first NHL season. Although the Flames had drafted him in 1980, Loob chose to stay with Farjestads BK for four seasons in his native Sweden. Fans had wondered how the slight 175-pound winger, generously listed at five-foot-nine, would handle the rough stuff in the NHL. But Loob was on his way to pro-ducing 30 goals and 23 assists to earn a spot on the NHL's all-rookie team.

Joel Otto, a hulking six-foot-four and 220-pound centre was another free agent signing from an American college. Many reporters and fans had never heard of Bemidji State, a National Collegiate Athletic Association (NCAA) Division II school in Otto's home state of Minnesota. If it was hard for Division I players to reach the NHL, it was twice as hard for Division II players. Although the NCAA is known for its large schools, like the University of Michigan and the UCLA, it also contains much smaller schools like Bemidji. Few scouts in any sport, let alone hockey, which is considered a regional game in the U.S., ever set foot on campus.

Winger Tim Hunter, a native of Calgary, was known more for his fighting ability than his scoring talent, but he had also worked hard and managed to impress Johnson. After being drafted by Atlanta in 1979, and spending one more year of major junior and two more in the minors, he was finally getting his chance to stick with the Flames.

Defenceman Jamie Macoun was yet another undraft-ed player from the U.S. college ranks. After joining the Flames midway through his third season with the Ohio State Buckeyes, in 1982-83, the native of Newmarket, Ontario, did not play a single game in the minors.

And then there was Doug Risebrough. As a 20-year-old rookie in 1974, Risebrough had managed to capture one of the two open roster spots on the most talented teams in NHL history, the Montreal Canadiens. With them, he won four straight Stanley Cups. In hockey parlance, Risebrough was a grinder — a player put out specifically to stop the other team's best players. After being traded to the Flames, he also emerged as a leader — by playing through several knee injuries. "I guess I'm a bit accident-prone, but I open myself up to it," said Risebrough, who played with a knee brace. "When you play at a certain level, you get hurt. Being injury-free is an insult . . . When you're not aching, maybe you're not doing the right things out there."

Calgary's goaltending situation was still uncertain. Reggie Lemelin was having an average year and Marc D'Amour, who suffered from severe dehydration during games, had not panned out as a backup. Calgary native Mike Vernon, an up-and-coming pro who had spent most of the season in the minors, appeared to be in the coach's doghouse. He had publicly challenged Johnson, contending the coach was not giving him a fair shot. Johnson said Vernon would have to earn his playing time. Eventually, Vernon would leave Johnson no other choice but to play him, because he played better than Calgary's other masked men. In 18 games, the young goaltender posted a 9-3-3 record.

Thanks to the unheralded young players and the veteran Risebrough, Calgary's 11-game losing streak became a distant memory.

The Flames placed sixth overall in the 1985-86 season,

but still finished 30 points behind the Oilers' juggernaut. Edmonton finished first overall, thanks to Gretzky's 215 points and 48 goals from Paul Coffey, the most by a defenceman in one season. Edmonton also owned the Battle of Alberta. The Flames had only managed to beat their rivals once — late in the season — as they romped to a 9-3 decision. It was an important victory because the Flames knew that if they were going to advance very far in the playoffs they would have to beat the two-time defending Stanley Cup champions.

The all-Alberta series of the second round started on a hilarious note at Northlands Coliseum in Edmonton. In the first period, rookie defenceman Gary Suter's expensive aluminum stick flew into the stands. Al Murray, a Calgary assistant trainer, jumped into the stands to get it. Edmonton fans refused to give it back and he got into a scuffle. From the bench, head medical trainer "Bearcat" Murray saw his son getting punched so he climbed over the glass to help him. Jumping down about eight feet, he landed awkwardly on a step and injured his ankle. As he was rolled out on a stretcher to an ambulance, a TV photographer followed him. Bearcat, easily recognizable by his bald head and bushy moustache, blew kisses at the camera. The Bearcat legend was born. After being fitted with a cast with a special spiked shoe to help him walk on the ice, he went back behind the Calgary bench for the second period.

Fans watching the game on TV in Boston were so impressed by Murray's courageous and successful efforts to retrieve Suter's stick that they launched the Bearcat Murray Fan Club! Whenever Bearcat would visit a rink in Boston, Montreal, or Quebec City, his faithful followers would don skull caps, fake noses, and moustaches. The native of High River, Alberta, who had inherited his nickname from his father, became the only trainer in the NHL with his own groupies.

Back on the ice, the cocky Vernon emerged as the starter ahead of Lemelin as the Flames and Oilers went back and forth until game seven on April 30, 1986 at Northlands Coliseum. With the score tied 2-2 and only about seven minutes to go in the third period, Calgary's Perry Berezan shot the puck along the boards. Edmonton goaltender Grant Fuhr went behind the net to stop it. Rookie Edmonton defenceman Steve Smith raced back to get it. But as Fuhr was returning to his net, Smith tried to fire the puck up ice —through the crease. The disk hit the back of Fuhr's leg — and caromed into the net. Smith fell to the ice and buried his face in shame as the Oilers' faithful went silent. Finally, he got up with tears streaming down his face. The goal was credited to Berezan, who was on the bench by that time. The Flames held on to win the game and the series. For the first time ever, Calgary eliminated Edmonton in the post-season. But the Flames did not just upset their rivals — they derailed an impending dynasty.

In the semi-finals, Calgary faced St. Louis and ex-Flames Eddy Beers, Gino Cavallini, and Charlie Bourgeois. Again the series went to seven games as St. Louis goaltender Rick Wamsley delivered a masterful performance. But Calgary prevailed again — and advanced to the Stanley Cup finals for the first time in its franchise's history. At last, McDonald was going to get a shot at the Cup. For the first time since 1967, the final pitted two Canadian teams against each other: Calgary vs. Montreal.

Like Badger, Montreal Canadiens coach Jean Perron had also elected to go with a rookie goaltender. Patrick Roy, a rakish Quebec City native, had racked up an impressive 11-4 record so far in the playoffs. In front of Roy, the Canadiens had some players from their halcyon days, but whose careers were then coming to a close — Bob Gainey, Larry Robinson, and the injured Mario Tremblay. The Habs also featured several promising young players, such as Guy Carbonneau, Chris Chelios, and rookies Claude Lemieux and Brian Skrudland.

The Flames, aside from the aging McDonald and injury-riddled Risebrough, were a young, inexperienced team. Most players were still in their 20s. By finishing ahead of the Habs in the regular season, Calgary had home-ice advantage in the final. The Flames controlled the first game, winning 5-3 at the Saddledome. Their chances of victory were also looking good in the second game as they remained tied 2-2 heading into overtime.

Then something bizarre happened. On the opening face-off, Skrudland grabbed a loose puck, raced toward Vernon on a breakaway and scored — just nine seconds into

O.T. It was the fastest overtime goal in NHL history.

The Flames never recovered. Montreal took both games at the Forum as future hall-of-famer Roy earned his first NHL playoff shutout. The teams returned to Calgary, and the Canadiens won 4-3 to capture the Cup.

After the game, Lanny McDonald slumped beside his locker in the Flames dressing room. As the cameras clicked and rolled, he did all he could to hold back his tears as he answered reporters' questions. Teammates and fans alike hoped that somehow, some way, the Flames would win the Cup for their beloved Lanny. McDonald just hoped that his team would get back into the finals — and give him one more chance — before he retired.

Chapter 4
A New Era

Calgary's 1987-88 training camp was full of hype. A year had passed since the Flames' improbable run to the final. Unfortunately, Winnipeg had stunned Calgary in the first round of the next season. Coach Bob Johnson had resigned suddenly to head up the governing body of hockey in the U.S. so Terry Crisp, Calgary's former farm club coach, was now running the bench. He had several tough decisions to make because several rookies were vying for jobs. Reporters wondered who would steal the show this year.

Would it be Brett Hull, the son of former Chicago superstar Bobby, whom Crisp had coached in the minors? Or former Cornell University centre Joe Nieuwendyk who had been the draft pick Calgary acquired for Kent Nilsson? Maybe tough-guy Gary Roberts? One of the goaltending prospects? The answer was none of the above. It turned out to be someone they least expected, but someone who also knew all about challenges.

He swaggered into town like he owned the place. The team listed him at five-foot-five and 153 pounds, but he insisted that he was actually five-foot-six and 158 pounds. His name was Theoren Fleury, a 19-year-old who grew up in Russell, Manitoba, just across the provincial border from his birthplace of Oxbow, Saskatchewan.

The previous Christmas, Fleury had been involved in one of the most infamous incidents in international junior hockey history. At Piestany, Czechoslovakia, which became known as the Piestany Punch Up, Canada's junior team squared off against the Soviets. Fleury was Team Canada's captain and — living up to his reputation as an agitator — became involved in a scuffle that erupted into a bench-clearing brawl. The Soviets did not, as a rule, drop their gloves, so this action alone was quite amazing. It got worse. Unable to control the mayhem, the officials left the ice. Tournament organizers finally brought the situation under control — 20 minutes later — by dimming the lights. The game was cancelled, both teams were disqualified, and their records erased from the tournament's official statistics.

At best, Fleury was supposed to be a long shot to make the Flames team that year or any other year. Calgary had selected him in the eighth round of the 1987 draft. Fletcher would claim years later that the farm team had needed an attraction that could help sell tickets. But Fleury quickly gained notice from the big club because of the way he took on much bigger players. "My size gives me more incentive to play hard," Fleury said. "The quote I always use is, 'Big guys prove they can't play. Little guys prove they can.'"

Coach Crisp gave him a chance to prove himself against the Chicago Blackhawks in an exhibition game, assigning him to check top scorer Denis Savard. Afterwards, Fleury acted like a kid who had just been given a lifetime supply of computer games. "It was a big thrill being on the ice with Savard," he said. "The heart was pumping. I thought, 'Holy cow, that's Denis Savard! He's a very exciting player, like myself."

That cocky attitude did not endear Fleury to veteran Flames, with whom he sparred in workouts. However Fletcher and the coaches raved about his willingness to get physical and about his offensive talent. Fletcher called him the best player for his size that he had ever seen, based on his ability to combine his antagonistic style with pure offensive skills. "Before camp, I'd have said it was highly unlikely," said Fletcher, about Fleury's hopes of ever playing in the NHL. "Now, I'm prepared to say that he has a pretty good chance."

That comment could be interpreted another way. It also meant that Fletcher was willing, in the future, to make moves that would get Fleury into the lineup. But at the end of the training camp, he was sent back to his junior team in

Moose Jaw for one more season. "I've proven I can play in this league," said Fleury. "I'm going down with the intention of being the best player in the Western Hockey League. I couldn't be happier. I had a great camp."

Although they did not take camp by storm the way Fleury did, two other rookies also impressed Fletcher and the coaching staff. Nieuwendyk stayed with the team after camp ended and started his NHL career on a scoring tear. Not bad considering that he had been ignored as a prospect when he was in midget. The Ontario Hockey Association, now known as the Ontario Hockey League, selected its players in an annual midget draft. Since no teams chose Nieuwendyk, he made his way to Cornell University in Ithaca, New York. There he grew a few inches and put on more weight, making him difficult to move from in front of the net. He was the East Coast Athletic Conference's rookie of the year in 1984-85 and a two-time first all-star. The Flames managed not to miss this prospect: they drafted Nieuwendyk in the second round of the NHL draft in 1985.

The other rookie star of the training camp was Nieuwendyk's best friend from their days growing up in Whitby, Ontario, Gary Roberts. The very physical Roberts soon made up for the absence of Risebrough who had retired and become an assistant coach because of knee and shoulder injuries. While Nieuwendyk had taken the U.S. college route to the NHL, Roberts took the major junior route with the Ottawa 67s and Guelph Platers, winning Memorial Cups

A New Era

with both teams. After leaving Whitby as a teenager, when he was still in high school, Roberts had trouble adjusting to life in Ottawa. Because he was a hockey player, he was often challenged to fight in his new school. But his Ottawa coach Brian Kilrea had invoked a strict no-fighting policy for Roberts, at least off the ice. One day, in a classroom with a teacher present, Roberts did get into a fight. Fearing the worst, he told Kilrea what happened. After getting confirmation from the teacher that the other boy had started the fight, Kilrea allowed Roberts to stay with the team. Roberts learned to control his fiery temper and became one of Ottawa's best players as well as a Calgary first-round draft pick in 1984.

Reunited after a few years of playing apart, Roberts and Nieuwendyk both quickly became comfortable at the NHL level. By December 29, after Calgary stomped Montreal 9-3, Nieuwendyk already had four hat-tricks. "If somebody told me I'd have 26 goals by the halfway mark, I wouldn't have believed it," said Nieuwendyk. "I don't feel any pressure." His new coach joked, "We're going to keep him around for a while. We're not going to send him to the minors. We'll probably take a little longer look at the kid."

Coach Crisp was not nearly as enamoured with his club's backup goaltender. Doug Dadswell, a free agent signing from Cornell, had assumed the job. But Dadswell did not inspire confidence in Crisp — or GM Fletcher. The GM went looking for a veteran backup. He called up St. Louis Blues general manager Ron Caron, with whom he had worked in

47

the Montreal and St. Louis organizations. Fletcher and Caron had worked out the Mullen deal the previous season.

Although Fletcher had appeared to have fleeced him in the Mullen deal, Caron was willing to trade with his old friend again. Caron wanted one player in particular — Brett Hull. The winger was off to a hot start in his first full NHL season with 50 points in 52 games. But, Fletcher reasoned, the Flames had plenty of offence. Nieuwendyk was on a roll — and the promising Theoren Fleury was in a race for the Western Hockey League scoring lead with Joe Sakic of the Swift Current Broncos. So, Fletcher completed the deal.

Hull would become one of the most prolific goal scorers in NHL history and snare at least three Stanley Cups. "We knew he was going to be a scorer, but we didn't know how good a scorer he was going to be," said Crisp. Crisp maintained that the deal made sense at the time because it provided Calgary with what it needed — more goaltending and defence. In return for Hull and utility forward Steve Bozek, Fletcher obtained goaltender Rick Wamsley, who had impressed Calgary the year the Flames advanced to the Stanley Cup final, and Rob Ramage, a solid defenceman who also stood out in that series.

Keeping tabs on his former club's recruiting prowess, Fletcher knew that Wamsley had started his NHL career with the Habs, where one season he shared the William Jennings Trophy with Denis Herron for best team goals-against average. The GM also knew that Wamsley didn't wobble when facing adversity. While he was with Montreal, Wamsley's son Ryan had died of cancer. In his memory, Wamsley helped fund a special room for cancer patients. Whenever he travelled to Montreal, he visited the room and paid tribute to his late son. Wamsley turned out to be steady, although not spectacular, as a backup to Vernon, who enjoyed his finest career year as a pro.

Nieuwendyk finished with a rookie record of 51 goals, surpassing the previous mark of 50 set by Islanders star Mike Bossy, to easily win the league's rookie of the year award. For the first time in franchise history, Calgary finished first overall, even better than the dreaded Oilers.

But after easily eliminating the Los Angeles Kings in four games, the Flames were swept 4-0 by the Oilers, who went on to win their fourth Cup in five years.

Now, as the Flames prepared for the 1988-89 season, fans and media alike started to question the team's character. What would it take to win the Cup?

Chapter 5
Chasing the
Stanley Cup

Doug Gilmour joined the Flames at the start of their 1988-89 training camp — but not by choice. The St. Louis Blues shipped Gilmour to Calgary in a package deal mainly because the parents of a 14-year-old girl who babysat his daughter had filed a $1 million lawsuit against him. The babysitter's parents alleged that he had molested her. The lawsuit proceeded, even though a grand jury decided there was insufficient evidence to lay charges. Even St. Louis prosecuting attorney George Westfall suggested the whole affair smacked of extortion.

Blues chairman Mike Shanahan later admitted that trading Gilmour "broke [GM] Ron Caron's heart." But, said

Shanahan, the deal had to be done to get Gilmour out from under intense public scrutiny — and let the team get back to business. "The trade wasn't based on the normal circumstances to improve your team, and that bothered us most of all," said Shanahan. Bullard, the key player going the other way, would play only 20 games with St. Louis. Craig Coxe would play only half a season there. Tim Corkery would stay in college that season.

Fortunately, the controversy did not affect Gilmour's play. He had faced misfortune before. When Gilmour was 16, his cousin Michael Anson, only a year younger, had died of cancer. "In a matter of two years he wasted away until nothing was left of him," Gilmour recalled. "I've never forgotten that. It made me realize how important life is." Gilmour also faced obstacles because of his size while growing up in Kingston, Ontario, a hometown he shared with one of his boosters, broadcaster Don Cherry. Although he was listed in NHL records as 5-foot-11 and 170 pounds, Gilmour always appeared to be shorter and slighter. During each game, he sweated off several pounds and often became dehydrated. As a result, he was not expected to be a star when he played for the Cornwall Royals of the Ontario Hockey League. "He was so small, he would just barely make a lot of teams as he was growing up," said Gordie Wood, a scout for the Royals. "But the people who figured that forgot about his heart. He just never let anything stop him."

Gilmour surprised his critics by being selected the

OHL's player of the year in 1982-83 as he compiled 70 goals and led the league with 107 assists and 177 points. However, he was not drafted into the NHL until the seventh round. Dismayed by the Blues' offer, he fled to West Germany, thinking he might play there. The Blues lured him back with a better deal within days. He made the club right away and did not play a single game in the minors. In his first three seasons in St. Louis, he was perceived as a checker, because he never produced more than 57 points. In 1986-87, his offensive output exploded to 107 points and he followed that up with 86 and 85-point seasons.

As the 1988-89 season began, Gilmour was viewed as a saviour, someone who could help the Flames take their final step to the top of the mountain. The Flames faced intense pressure to make up for their early exit the previous season. Calgary also had an image to live up to.

Since coming to Calgary, the Flames had never missed the playoffs. It was now a given that the Flames would make the playoffs every year. The only question was how far they would advance in the post-season. Flames supporters had come to expect excellence. Calgary had also become known as a good place to play.

Calgary was a "small-market franchise" because the city's population was tiny compared to cities like New York and Boston. Since the Flames had fewer potential fans, the team could not attract as much TV revenue with which to pay huge salaries to superstars. Despite this, players from other teams still welcomed trades to Calgary because they knew that general manager Fletcher would treat them well. But Coach Crisp was wary of his team becoming too comfortable. He knew that his players were making a lot more money than he did when he was playing. Calgary also had an experienced team and veterans on one-way contracts could earn just as much playing in the minors as in the NHL, so there was no financial incentive for them to perform at their best. Crisp was afraid that they would not play as well as they could play.

With Gilmour in the lineup, the Flames started the 1988-89 season slowly with a 4-4 tie at home with the New York Islanders and a 6-5 overtime loss in Los Angeles. Then Calgary racked up five wins and a tie in their next six games. In addition to Gilmour, several other players were starting to shine — including centre Jiri Hrdina and Jamie Macoun.

Hrdina had joined the Flames after the 1988 Winter Olympics in Calgary. Although Czechoslovakia was still a communist nation and residents were not allowed to move to other countries, Fletcher negotiated Hrdina's release from his former team and gained permission for him to come to Canada. At the age of 30, because he had not played more than 25 games the previous season, Hrdina was the NHL's oldest rookie. Politics and age aside, his arrival in the NHL was amazing because the native of Mlada Boleslav had struggled to earn a spot with the Czechoslovakian national squad.

Meanwhile, Macoun was back after missing the entire 1987-88 season following a controversial accident. Losing control of his sports car, he had suffered a broken and nerve-damaged arm, as well as internal injuries and severe cuts. He was initially charged with drinking and driving, but pled guilty to a lesser charge of dangerous driving and paid a $1,000 fine. He had to submit to alcohol counselling and underwent extensive rehabilitation on his injured arm. The damage to his reputation may have been worse. The story splashed across the sports news and many questioned whether he was getting off too lightly. But Macoun showed no signs of any recurring problems and played regularly.

Macoun's return gave Calgary one of the strongest defence corps in the NHL. MacInnis, with his booming shot, and Suter, the NHL's rookie of the year in 1985-86, made Calgary's No. 1 power play unit one of the best in the league. Gilmour was scoring at a steady pace while team scoring leader Joe Mullen was near the top of the league in both goals and assists. Hakan Loob, MacInnis, and Suter were all producing at a healthy clip.

Meanwhile, down south in Salt Lake, Fleury, in his first full pro season, was constantly turning the red light on. After taking Calgary's training camp by storm the previous season, Fleury had gone back to Moose Jaw, captained Canada to a gold medal during a much more peaceful world junior championships, and completed his junior eligibility with Moose Jaw. Tying Joe Sakic of the Swift Current Broncos for the Western League scoring title, Fleury had lived up to his bold prediction that he would be the best player on the junior circuit.

Off the ice, Fleury was learning how to be a teenage father to his infant son, Josh, after girlfriend Shannon Griffin had given birth a few months earlier. It wasn't the first or the last of Fleury's challenges in life. He was in the early stages of a substance abuse problem, which would haunt him years later. Although it wasn't known at the time, his parents had also suffered from addictions. And, as it turned out, his former junior coach, Graham James, had also sexually abused players when Fleury was still in junior. James would be convicted of his crimes years later. If Fleury had been aware of some of the coach's activities, he had not let on.

Fleury signed with the Flames in time to join their farm club in Salt Lake for the American League playoffs. He counted eight goals in only 11 games and helped the Golden Eagles claim the Calder Cup championship, while also earning the playoff MVP honours. After attending his second Calgary training camp, he was sent back to Salt Lake because, unlike the veterans, he was on a two-way deal that paid him less in the minors.

As Fleury began the season in the minors, the Flames got off to a slow start with their new star Gilmour. They quickly rebounded. In their first 16 games, they only lost three times. Later they launched a 13-game undefeated streak, allaying Crisp's earlier fears that they would become complacent and not try their hardest. But, around Christmas time, Calgary went into the doldrums. After losing only four times in their first 46 outings, the Flames had only four wins in their last 10 games. The poor showings posed additional concern because, with the exception of Montreal, they all came against Smythe Division rivals — teams that they would have to beat in the first two rounds, often the toughest, of the playoffs.

The Flames needed someone who could shake them out of their lethargy, someone who could lift the team offensively if necessary and provide the grit that appeared to be lacking. Crisp and Fletcher knew exactly where to find him. On the first day of 1989, the Flames called up Fleury. "We were look-ing for some kind of spark," recalled Crisp. "We had a lot of good pieces in place. He was playing so well in the minors. He was a bottle of energy. He made things go."

Flames management personnel, said Crisp, wanted to find out whether Fleury was any good or whether they were just wasting their time trying to develop him into an NHLer. "He was a little buzz bomb," said Crisp. "He'd go out and stir up the hornet's nest and he could make things happen." The pesky forward, who could play both centre and wing, con-tinued his high-scoring ways in the NHL. He saw action on the power play and penalty killing units while also taking a regular shift.

The Flames had their answer. Fleury was there to stay. Someone else's job was in jeopardy. "What he did was, he made everybody accountable," said Crisp. The Flames lost a total of only six games in January and February. In addition to Fleury and the other stars, so-called lesser lights such as Otto, Patterson, Peplinski, Tim Hunter, and Mark Hunter were also providing timely goals. But one veteran was struggling. His name was Lanny McDonald.

It was widely believed that this would be McDonald's final season in the NHL, although he was not ready to confirm his retirement plans. His offence had declined steadily in recent years and his nagging injuries were catching up with him. At the beginning of the season, McDonald had appeared to be a shoe-in to garner two milestones — his 500th goal and his 1000th career point. As February turned into March, he still had not attained them.

Coach Crisp was naturally not concerned about a player's personal achievements. He was only concerned about his team's achievements. So, on many nights, McDonald sat in the press box while his younger teammates played. "That's probably the hardest and toughest thing you'll do as a coach, when you have the character of the guys who have earned the right to be there," said Crisp.

Unlike many of his rival coaches, Crisp had a deep and talented lineup. He merely tried to put in the right players at the right time. McDonald kept working hard in practice, and in early March, the coach put him back into games. On March 7, 1989, he collected his 1,000th career point as he scored two goals in a 9-5 win over Winnipeg. On March 21, against the

New York Islanders, he carried the puck behind the net and scored his 500th career goal on a wraparound.

But there was still one prize that McDonald was missing. The Stanley Cup.

Meanwhile, Fletcher and Crisp felt the team was also missing something. Although the Flames had plenty of scorers, and a steady goaltender in Vernon, they did not have enough checkers for the GM's or the coach's liking. With 12 games left in the regular season, while McDonald was chasing his milestones, Fletcher acquired winger Brian MacLellan from the Minnesota North Stars.

Again, Fletcher had plucked a player who had overcome many odds to reach the NHL — and who was playing beyond anyone's expectations of him. Growing up in Guelph, Ontario, MacLellan started playing hockey later than most of his friends. While his buddies were skating, MacLellan was in a leg brace, suffering from Legg-Perthes disease, a condition that attacks the hip joint. Doctors later recommended that he start playing hockey because exercise and the cool, moist arena air might improve the condition. MacLellan joined a house league team in Guelph and worked intensely on his game. The hip never bothered him again. He grew to six-foot-three and earned many offers from U.S. colleges. He opted to attend Ohio's Bowling Green University, where he was named to the All-American team in all four years of his college eligibility. No NHL team drafted him. In 1982, the Kings took a chance and signed him as a free agent.

Over the next two years, on a line with Marcel Dionne, MacLellan scored 25 and 31 goals, respectively. Mid-way through his fourth season in L.A., MacLellan was traded to the Rangers. After he fell out of favour with coach Ted Sator because he refused to play a more physical style, New York sent MacLellan to Minnesota. The North Stars were able to tap MacLellan's potential in 1986-87 and he produced 32 goals and added 31 assists.

Like McDonald, MacLellan knew that his NHL days were numbered. He was already taking college courses off-season to prepare for a business career after his playing days. So far in his seven-year career, MacLellan's teams had only made the playoffs twice. For the previous three seasons, the North Stars had not qualified for the post-season. At last, like McDonald, he was going to get his shot at the Cup.

The Flames finished the regular season with a 54-17-9 record — one of the best in modern NHL history. They were assured of home-ice advantage, meaning they would host the first two games and the seventh game, if necessary, of each series. In other words, Calgary was the obvious favourite to win Lord Stanley's mug. The pressure was on.

Calgary drew the Canucks in the opening round. After finishing fourth in the Smythe Division, Vancouver was not expected to do much in the post-season, but coach Bob McCammon was not nicknamed "Cagey" for nothing. He had earned the moniker for using his brain rather than his brawn while playing and coaching in the tough International

League. Much to the delight of reporters, he was also quick with colourful quotes, which he used as barbs to upset his team's opponents. As a former Oilers assistant, he was a veteran of the Battle of Alberta, so he liked to claim, "Cliff Fletcher built his team to beat Edmonton. Now he's got a big team that plays tough and doesn't know how else to play."

In the first game, former Flame Paul Reinhart scored at 2:47 of overtime to give the Canucks a 4-3 victory at the Saddledome. The Flames countered with a 5-2 decision in game two, tying the series as it shifted to the West Coast. The Flames subdued the Pacific Coliseum crowd by blanking the Canucks 4-0 in the third game, but Vancouver took the fourth game, 5-3. Back in Calgary, Vernon posted his second shutout of the series in the fifth game as the Flames won 4-0 and took a 3-2 lead in games.

Before game six, Cagey again accused the Flames of succeeding because they were goons, rather than talented players who capitalized on their skills. "They're trying to make it like they're the Cinderella of this thing." The Canucks rode the barb and the hot goaltending of Kirk McLean to a 6-3 victory in Vancouver in the sixth game, setting the stage for a dramatic seventh and deciding contest at the Saddledome on April 15, 1989.

The upstart Canucks had forced the Flames to a seventh game. Now, it was Vernon's turn to shine. Among his more memorable saves, he foiled Stan Smyl on a breakaway, picking off his hard wrist shot with his trapper mitt. He also forced Tony Tanti to hit the post on a wraparound and barely got his toe on a Petri Skriko slapshot. Thanks to Vernon, the score was tied 3-3 after regulation time. With less than a minute to go in the first overtime period, Peplinski skated with the puck along the right-wing boards and fired it at the net as Otto tangled with Canucks defenceman Harold Snepsts. Although Otto had his back to Peplinski, the puck hit Otto's skate and somehow went in, giving the Flames 4-3 wins in both the game and the series. "That was a heart-stopper," Crisp recalled in an understatement.

The tension increased as the Flames advanced to meet the Los Angeles Kings and a former foe from the Battle of Alberta — the dreaded Gretzky. In the opening game, Bearcat Murray almost caused a few coronaries himself. When Kings' sniper Bernie Nicholls decked Vernon, Murray hopped over the boards and raced to Vernon. Bearcat wore spiked shoes, which were designed to prevent him from slipping on the ice. They did not let him down and he arrived in Vernon's crease in a few seconds — but the whistle had not blown. "I think we're in trouble here," Bearcat told Vernon, pushing him to the safety of the back of the net and hoping the referee wouldn't see them. The play continued at the other end of the ice. A few moments later, MacInnis scored. The Kings players and coaches howled in protest, but the goal was allowed to stand. The Flames went on to win the game — despite Gretzky — and sweep the series. Except for Bearcat's shenanigans, the battle that many thought would go seven games was surprisingly without drama.

The Flames then advanced to the Clarence Campbell Conference finals against the Mike Keenan-coached Chicago Blackhawks. Calgary disposed of the Blackhawks in relatively easy fashion, taking the series 4-1. As co-captain McDonald held up the Clarence Campbell Trophy, the Saddledome chanted "Lanny! Lanny!" in a deafening roar. As he skated off the ice, sweat pouring from his playoff beard, spectators sensed that McDonald was making one of his last appearances. They were ecstatic that he would get another chance to put his name on the Cup. They still must have wondered, how much ice time would he get?

The Stanley Cup final series opened May 14, 1989. Calgary skated away with a 4-3 win. Montreal doubled Calgary 4-2 in the second game and the series headed to Montreal tied 1-1. Ryan Walter's goal in double overtime gave the hometown Habs a 4-3 decision and the series lead. The Flames rallied to beat Montreal 4-2 in game four at the Forum.

Back in Calgary, the Flames delighted the Saddledome faithful with a 3-2 victory, which also gave Crisp's crew a 3-2 series lead. For the third straight game, McDonald had watched from the press box. The series returned to Montreal, with Calgary on the verge of clinching its first Stanley Cup. Many wondered whether McDonald had already played his final game as a Flame. Would Crisp sit him out again?

In Montreal, Cliff Fletcher, showing a rarely seen superstitious side, had two other people on his mind — radio play-by-play announcer Peter Maher and his sidekick, colour commentator Doug Barkley. Maher had been calling the Flames action — home and away — since their second season in Calgary.

Hockey players, coaches, and managers can be creatures of habit. They will stick to the same routines if they think it brings them luck. On road trips, a team member will choose his seat on the team bus — and sit there every time. Before the bus leaves the hotel for the game, the manager checks to make sure that everyone is aboard simply by looking at their regular seats. Anyone missing is a cause for concern, because his absence could be a bad omen.

Maher and Barkley usually took the team bus to the rink. They also sat in the same seats to satisfy the superstitious. On the bus before game four in Montreal — which the Flames lost — Fletcher had noticed the absence of the broadcasters. Maher and Barkley had taken a cab to the Forum that time because media were staying at a different hotel.

Before game six, Fletcher had ordered Maher and Barkley to be on the bus. He did not want any part of the team's routine to change before such an important game. Although they again had a shorter route to the Forum from their own hotel, Maher and Barkley complied. They took a cab to the Flames' hotel to get on the bus. Earlier in the day, Maher had also snuck out and bought three tiny bottles of champagne — one for himself, one for his brother who would also be in the booth that night, and one for Barkley

— and slipped them into his bag. Would this be the night?

When the Flames came out for the opening face-off, McDonald was among the starters. McDonald even wore the captain's 'C'. Crisp stunned many observers by leaving co-captains Tim Hunter and Jim Peplinski out of the lineup. He did not feel that they were playing as well as they could and thought the Flames needed more offence than physical prowess that night.

At least McDonald was at least in uniform — rather than in the press box — for what was likely to be the final game of his career. But coach Crisp had more surprises — he inserted McDonald on a line with Nieuwendyk and Roberts. McDonald, knowing that each shift could be the last of his career, was flying from the start. It was obvious he wanted to remember this night forever.

The score was tied 1-1 after the first period. Early in the second, as a penalty to McDonald was expiring, Nieuwendyk carried the puck over centre ice towards the Montreal zone. McDonald raced out of the sin bin and joined the action. Nieuwendyk fired a shot on goal, but Roy kicked it out. McDonald zoomed in for the rebound and one-timed it past the startled Montreal netminder to give Calgary a 2-1 lead at 4:24. McDonald ecstatically lifted his arms above his head and danced in celebration. Wasn't it perfect, he mused. What might be his last goal as a Flame had come in the same rink as his first one.

The Habs came back to tie the score 2-2. In the third

Lanny McDonald holding the Stanley Cup.

period, Gilmour knocked in his own rebound and then added an empty-net goal to give the Flames a 4-2 victory — and their first Stanley Cup. And, for the first time ever, a visiting team had captured the Stanley Cup on Forum ice.

As the final horn sounded, Crisp, so relieved at having won, scaled the glass behind the bench into the first row of seats — and planted a kiss firmly on the lips of Al MacNeil's surprised wife Norma, while his own wife Sheila sat amused nearby. Up in the radio booth, Maher borrowed a line from a song by rock star Rod Stewart. "Yeah, baby!" Maher roared into the microphone. After handing out his hidden champagne to his brother and Barkley, Maher decided that "yeah, baby!" would be his signature phrase. He vowed to only use it on very special occasions.

Down on the ice, Hunter and Peplinski, still dressed in their red longjohns from watching the game in the dressing room, hoisted the Stanley Cup together. Owner Harley Hotchkiss looked on from the bench area. "Should I be out there?" Hotchkiss asked MacNeil. "You don't get this chance very often," said MacNeil. "Get out there!"

So the Calgary Flames — players, coaches, managers, trainers, and owners — assembled for a famous team photo, lying, sitting, or kneeling as they crowded into the shot. It was a moment they would remember for the rest of their lives. It was also their last time on ice together.

Chapter 6
Life After Gilmour

After he and Calgary won the Cup at last, McDonald retired during a gala party on the lawn of his home. Approximately 100 old friends came to say farewell, including the couple who billeted him while he played junior in Lethbridge. McDonald spoke to reporters from a wooden podium that was about a foot off the ground. Oblivious to the significance of the occasion, Lanny's five-year-old son amused himself by jumping on and off the wooden structure. He thumped here, there, and everywhere. Nobody — not even the radio reporters, whose clips were disrupted — seemed to mind.

But fans became perturbed when, in a more surprising move, Hakan Loob also quit the NHL. He returned to play in his homeland, Sweden, where he wanted his young children to attend school.

The Flames held their 1989-90 training camp in Moscow, one of the first NHL teams to do so, reflecting the modernization of communism in the former superpower. In the Flames lineup was Sergei Makarov, one of the first former soviet stars allowed to play in the NHL.

Changes to Calgary's lineup continued as the Flames returned to Calgary and began the regular season. After only six games, captain Jim Peplinski unexpectedly retired — at the age of 29 — because he no longer enjoyed pro hockey.

Despite these blows, Calgary still finished first overall in the 1989-90 season. But after the Los Angeles Kings stunned Calgary in the first-round of the playoffs, coach Crisp lost his job. He was surprised and upset, feeling that the team's top finish had earned him another season.

In 1990-91, under new coach Risebrough, the Flames placed a respectable fourth overall as Fleury potted a career-high 51 goals. But Calgary lost to the Edmonton Oilers in seven games —once again — and in the first round. After 19 years at the helm of the franchise, president and general manager Cliff Fletcher resigned to take on the challenges of the Toronto Maple Leafs. Risebrough became general manager, but kept his coaching duties. The following season brought catastrophe.

With salaries escalating rapidly throughout the league, many Flames — Gilmour in particular — had been complaining about their contracts. On January 1, with the Flames struggling, he walked out on the team, and demanded a trade.

The next day, Risebrough shipped him to the Leafs in the largest trade in NHL history. Ten players were involved. Popular backup goaltender Rick Wamsley and defencemen Macoun and Rick Nattress and prospect Kent Manderville went with Gilmour to Toronto. Journalists and fans alike felt that Fletcher had fleeced his old protégé Risebrough. Calgary received Gary Leeman, a former 50-goal scorer with Toronto, who was supposed to be Calgary's new saviour. He only produced two goals and seven assists in 29 games.

Risebrough was heavily criticized for trading Gilmour so soon after his walkout. Late in the regular season, after a humiliating 11-0 loss to the Canucks in Vancouver, Risebrough resigned as coach. Assistant coach Guy Charron was appointed interim head coach for the balance of the season, which was interrupted by a general players' strike. He managed to light a fire under Calgary's struggling veterans, posting a respectable 6-7-3 record. But, for the first time since coming to Calgary, the Flames missed the playoffs.

What a difference two years made for the Flames.

In the off-season, Risebrough went looking for a new permanent head coach. After taking his time, Risebrough finally hired Dave King, the coach and general manager of Canada's national team. In February, while the Flames had been struggling, King had guided Canada to an Olympic silver medal — Canada's first Games hardware since 1968. The accomplishment was particularly impressive because, in those days, the NHL did not interrupt its season so that its players could participate in the Olympics. Canada's silver medal squad consisted primarily of amateurs, NHL castoffs, and holdouts like centre Eric Lindros and goaltender Sean Burke. After King had developed their castoffs and prospects, NHL clubs routinely plucked the players.

Because his teams were always deficient talent-wise, King became a master strategist, especially against the Soviet Union, whom he regarded as the cat to Canada's pigeon. He taught young Canadian players to believe in themselves — and they thrived. "I've always believed that the most important thing in coaching is never to be critical of anything other than the performance of a person," said King. Unlike most NHL coaches, who had played in the league, King was a career coach. Thanks to King, Canada's national program became a model for the rest of the world.

After nine seasons at the Canadian team's helm, though, King longed to coach in the world's best league — the NHL. "In the NHL there's a danger," said King. "Your job is on the line all the time. Not many people can do it successfully. That draws you to it. It's difficult and a great challenge." His challenge with the Flames was to get them back to the playoffs.

Before King could get his feet wet in the 1992-93 season, bad luck struck the Flames again. In October, Nieuwendyk nailed Vernon with a shot in the head in practice. The goalie suffered a 15-stitch cut to his forehead and had to sit out five games.

In November, defenceman Al MacInnis experienced a Remembrance Day that he would rather forget. In a game at Hartford, MacInnis was racing back to his own end to retrieve the puck with Whalers' rookie Patrick Poulin in hot pursuit. As MacInnis picked up the puck in the corner, Poulin poked him in the back of the legs with his stick. With his legs spread wide, MacInnis lost his balance, wishboned into the boards, and suffered a dislocated hip. The injury threatened to end his career.

Shortly after doctors reinserted the hip bone into its socket, however, MacInnis began his rehabilitation. A few weeks later, he shed his crutches and began off-ice workouts. "I'm surprised to see him walking around," said Dale Tallon, who had also dislocated a hip while playing for Chicago and still walked with a limp. "It was the most painful injury I ever had." Baseball and football star Bo Jackson had suffered a similar injury, forcing him to retire from both sports prematurely. MacInnis managed to avoid poor blood flow, which would have caused the hip to degenerate, by swimming for 30 minutes a day, and completing hip exercises that simulated skating, riding a stationary bike, and lifting weights. He began skating in January — only seven weeks after the injury — and resumed playing a short time later. Was the Flames' luck turning around at last?

Then the Flames suffered another major blow in a game

against the Philadelphia Flyers. Their high-scoring Roberts suffered a broken blood vessel in his thigh from Flyers defenceman Gary Galley's knee. The Flames flew to Toronto after the game; Roberts left the plane on a wheelchair and immediately underwent surgery. This injury also threatened to end Roberts' career.

But something incredible happened while Roberts, MacInnis, and several other players were out with injuries. Calgary kept winning. Living up to his reputation as a master tactician and excellent teacher, King got the most out of several other players — grateful Flames who knew all about overcoming the odds.

Defenceman Frank Musil had defected from Czechoslovakia with his wife, a former tennis star, in time to join the NHL for the 1986-87 season. He was so determined to learn English that he enrolled in kindergarten classes. The six-foot-three and 215-pound Musil had made an interesting contrast to his five-year-old classmates!

Defenceman Jim Kyte, once one of the most feared fighters in the game, was the first legally deaf player to toil in the NHL. As a result of a hereditary nerve condition, the Ottawa native's hearing had declined steadily since he was three years old. Although he could speak, quite eloquently in fact, he learned sign language. During off-seasons, he worked with deaf and hearing-impaired children at special hockey camps.

Winger Ron Stern had been only a teenager when his

father, a Montreal restaurateur, was murdered in a gangland slaying. Stern, still playing junior hockey at the time, managed to overcome his grief and crack the Vancouver Canucks roster after a few seasons in the minors.

As the end of the regular season approached, thanks to the amazing gritty performances of these unsung heroes, Calgary was assured of a playoff berth. With Roberts still out, the Flames were getting most of their goals from Fleury, Robert Reichel, Suter and Nieuwendyk. If Calgary was going do anything in the post-season, more players would have to score.

Defensive defenceman Trent Yawney was hoping he could contribute. With five games to go in the regular season, Yawney was still looking for his first goal. "You know it's getting tough when your wife starts bugging you," said Yawney. He had almost scored in a 4-3 victory over the San Jose Sharks. But Otto got his stick on Yawney's slapshot and got credit for the goal. In the next four games, despite coming close several times, Yawney still could not score. The regular season finale, again against San Jose, was his last chance. With Roberts back in the lineup after missing more than a third of the season, he set up Yawney — and the defenceman finally scored. The Flames beat the Sharks 7-3 to finish ninth overall.

Calgary opened the post-season against Los Angeles — and Yawney scored again, and again, and again. Suddenly, after three games, he was one of the hottest Flames. Most of Calgary's regular top scorers could not turn the red light on.

Vernon had also suffered an ankle injury and only played parts of the last two games. Backup Jeff Reese struggled at times and the Kings took the series in six.

In 1993-94, Calgary captured the new Pacific Division's title. In the first round, they faced Vancouver — for the fifth time in 13 years. The Canucks blanked the Flames 5-0 in the first game. Vernon, heavily criticized for his play in the first game, stoned the Canucks over the next three games. Calgary took a 3-1 series lead back to the Saddledome. At last, Calgary's first-round playoff jinx appeared to be coming to an end. But the Canucks stunned the Flames by taking the next three games — all in overtime — to capture the series in seven games. Pavel Bure's decisive breakaway goal spelled Vernon's departure. In June 1994, 13 years after he joined the Flames as a draft choice, he was traded to the Detroit Red Wings for defenceman Steve Chiasson. A couple of days later, Calgary traded MacInnis to St. Louis for defenceman Phil Housley, while the clubs also swapped draft picks.

As a result of the deals, most of the players from Calgary's Stanley Cup-winning squad were gone. The Flames once dreamed of becoming a dynasty but now they would have to win with a different cast of players.

Chapter 7
Iginla Arrives

I t was the fall of 1995 — and Calgary fans were staying away in droves. They were angry. The previous spring, the regular season had been reduced to 48 games because of a lockout. San Jose's goal, in the third overtime period in the seventh game, eliminated the Flames in the first round of the playoffs — once again. Fans were fed up with millionaire hockey players who griped about low salaries, while average players earned more than Lanny McDonald did in his heyday. Bad trades were also coming back to haunt the Flames. Although three years had passed since Gilmour's departure, it still rankled the Flames' faithful followers.

General manager Risebrough responded by firing coach

King in the off-season.

Risebrough became persona non grata. Griping about him in letters to the editor and on radio talk shows, fans wanted him out. One more bad trade, and one more bad season, they thought, and the financially struggling Flames could be forced to move out of Calgary.

The owners did not heed the fans' wishes — but they didn't show much faith in Risebrough either. In a bizarre move, they promoted assistant general manager Al Coates to a vice-president's post. In other words, Risebrough's underling became his boss. It certainly appeared as if Risebrough's job was in jeopardy.

Risebrough had managed to sign Fleury after he held out in training camp, but the troubled GM failed to ink Joe Nieuwendyk to a new agreement. The Calgary captain stayed away from camp, too, and when the regular season began, he demanded a trade or a new contract. Based on his offensive production throughout his career, he was due to earn about $5 million per season. The Flames could not afford to keep him. They could also not afford to surrender him without getting a decent player in return. Fans became even more livid. Nieuwendyk's holdout was reminding them of the Gilmour dispute, and everyone knew what had happened then. Risebrough refused to budge — so Nieuwendyk sat and waited.

The Flames started terribly under new coach Pierre Page, posting only one victory in their first 11 games. When the season — and Nieuwendyk's contract impasse — stretched into November, new vice-president Coates decided it was time to act. He fired his former boss Risebrough and took over as the club's GM. In December, with the Flames still playing terribly, Coates traded Nieuwendyk to the Dallas Stars. In return, Calgary obtained utility forward Corey Millen. They also got a junior prospect who played for the Kamloops Blazers and was preparing to suit up for Canada's junior team for the upcoming world championships in Boston. His name was Jarome Iginla.

In addition to excelling at hockey, Iginla was the starting catcher on Canada's national junior baseball team. One of the few black players in hockey, Iginla had grown up in an Edmonton suburb. Although his Nigerian-born father and Canadian mother divorced when he was a baby, Iginla maintained close relationships with both parents and enjoyed a happy and prosperous childhood in St.Albert.

St. Albert was also the hometown of former Oilers' star Mark Messier. Like Messier, his idol, Iginla could handle the rough going and he was a prolific scorer. Although he was often subject to racist remarks on the ice as opponents tried to throw him off his game, he had made the Kamloops lineup as a 16-year-old and already helped the Blazers win two Memorial Cup titles.

His trade to Calgary during the world juniors in Boston generated considerable buzz, because many journalists were present. Despite the attention surrounding him, Iginla thrived during the tournament. With five goals and seven assists in only seven games, he led Canada to the gold medal. Iginla returned to the Western League following the tournament and continued to score frequently. He finished the season as the Western League's fourth leading scorer with 63 goals and 73 assists and was named the player of the year.

Meanwhile, the Flames were making a late-season surge, thanks to the return of Roberts from an ongoing neck injury. He played only 35 games but still finished as Calgary's fifth top scorer with 20 goals and 22 assists. His courageous comeback would earn him the Masterton Trophy for perseverance and dedication to hockey. More importantly, it helped the Flames secure a playoff berth as they placed 15th overall. (Playoff seedings were now based on overall standings rather than divisional results.)

The Flames faced the Chicago Blackhawks in the playoffs — and promptly lost the first two games. By then the Kamloops' Blazers season was over, so general manager Coates called Iginla. While most of his teammates were sleeping in after a night of partying, 18-year-old Iginla flew to Calgary, signed a contract, and played that same night. Wearing No. 24 rather than his now familiar No. 12, Iginla notched his first NHL goal and an assist in his first two pro games. Rookies were generally considered lucky to start in regular season games, but Iginla played a regular shift in the post-season. Fleury was so impressed that he said the kid could play on his line any time.

Iginla Arrives

In spite of Iginla's help, the Flames were still eliminated in four straight games. They had not advanced beyond the first round of the playoffs since their 1988-89 Stanley Cup championship. The following three seasons came and went in a blur as the Flames reached new levels of futility and missed the playoffs every year. Iginla proved to be a gem among cobblestones as he led all rookies with 50 points in his first full pro season. However, even he slumped through his sophomore campaign.

As for the rest of the team, faces kept changing. Roberts retired for a year and then came out of retirement following neck surgery. He was traded to Hartford where he hoped his travel miles — and the risk of re-injuring his neck — would be reduced.

Fleury was now the only player remaining from Calgary's Stanley Cup-winning team. He was also among the highest-paid players in the NHL and would soon be seeking a new deal. Everyone knew that it was just a matter of time before, he, too, would be traded because the team could not afford to pay him a huge salary. There was more pressure than ever on the organization to find young players who could help the Flames regain their respect — and challenge the league's best for the Cup.

Page lasted one more season and then Brian Sutter took his place as coach. And, in February 1999, Coates traded Fleury to the Colorado Avalanche in a package deal. The key player coming to Calgary had yet to play in the NHL. He was an 18-year-old defenceman who had also played with the Kamloops Blazers — Robyn Regehr.

Although he was a Canadian citizen, Regehr had spent his early childhood in Brazil, where he was born, and Indonesia, as his parents served as international aid workers. As a result, he only started playing hockey when his family returned to their roots in Rosthern, Saskatchewan. Despite the late start, the game came naturally to Robyn. He made the Blazers as a 16-year-old and was also selected to Canada's team for the world junior championships. After the Flames had lost so many of their veteran defencemen, they viewed him as a blue-chip prospect.

On July 4, 1999, Regehr's pro career literally came crashing to a halt in a horrific car accident that was not his fault. He suffered terrible damage to his legs, the keys to his hockey career. A two-inch bolt was driven through the bone of his right knee as the floorboard, rendered jagged by the impact, had impaled his legs onto the seat. Both of his legs were broken. After doctors inserted rods in both legs, Regehr lay on his bed, looked up at the ceiling and prayed. "The main thing I tried to do was look at the positives of the situation. I was still alive," he said.

Regehr would not be able to skate for at least four to six months. Calgary's promising prospect would be lucky to play at all, let alone in the NHL. But his legs healed faster than anyone thought they would. By September, he was ready to get back on the ice — and he went to Calgary's training camp. He signed a contract with the Flames and went down to Calgary's farm team in St. John, New Brunswick, for a two-week conditioning stint. He played his first pro game only four months after his near-death experience.

On a Thursday night in the nation's capital, Regehr suited up for Calgary, giving meaning to a game too early in the regular season to count for anything else. Coach Brian Sutter said Regehr played a mistake-free game as the Flames prevailed 4-3 in overtime. "Sometimes things happen to make a person stronger," said Regehr. "I'm very appreciative of what I have now. I know things can change in an instant." The rebuilding Flames were also grateful to have him.

In the second half of the season, Fred Brathwaite became the Flame's inspiration. He was the sixth goaltender that the team used. Four others had suffered injuries and another one played only three games on an emergency basis. Calgary had actually signed Brathwaite, then a member of Canada's national team, to make up for a shortage of goalies on their farm team. After a disastrous road trip on which their goalies struggled, the Flames decided to bring in Brathwaite for a look-see. Brathwaite did not just emerge as the team's new starter — he posted the best goals against average in the NHL for a while. But Brathwaite's strong, sometimes spectacular, play still could not get the Flames into the playoffs. They failed to qualify for the post-season again the next year.

President Ron Bremner decided to clean house. General manager Coates, head coach Sutter, and assistant coach Rich

Preston were all fired. Although they had just tried to negotiate a trade for a top player — rumoured to be Gilmour — the owners vetoed it. The deal, said Sutter, would have propelled the Flames into the playoffs. Al MacNeil, who had served as an assistant coach under Sutter for three years, thought the head coach's dismissal was unfair. He too believed the Flames were on the verge of making the playoffs. Fed up with how far the Flames had fallen from their glory years, MacNeil quit the team in protest. Incredibly, the Flames' longest-serving and loyal employee was gone. And the Flames missed the playoffs again. Calgary handed the general manager's reins to Craig Button, a young executive from the Dallas Stars.

New coach Don Hay was fired with 13 games remaining in the regular season, and replaced by Greg Gilbert, a former assistant. The Flames missed the playoffs one more time. However, before the start of the next season, the owners asked Al MacNeil to return to the organization and resume his former role as a jack-of-all-trades executive. Again showing his loyalty, he quietly obliged after spending a year watching junior games and cleaning out his files at home.

Nonetheless, the Flames stumbled from the start and again failed to qualify for the 2000-01 post-season. Up in the radio booth, Peter Maher longed for the day when the Flames would give him something to yell "yeah baby" about again.

In June 2001, the Flames obtained goaltender Roman Turek in a deal that was viewed as a commitment to turning Calgary into a contender. The lanky goaltender from

Strakonice in the Czech Republic was soon due to become a free agent and would be in line for a salary in the $5-$6 million per year range. Turek's early success helped fans forget about their beloved Brathwaite, who went to St. Louis in the trade that brought the Czech goaltender to Calgary.

Calgary's owners also replaced President Bremner with Ken King, a former newspaper publisher. Acknowledging that he had no previous experience in pro hockey, King promised to let Button and his staff run the hockey side. He would concentrate on business operations. "It's about the hockey," said King, suggesting that the franchise's survival depended on a team that was successful on the ice.

For the first time in several seasons, Calgary zoomed out of the starting gate. Riding Turek's hot goaltending hand, the Flames posted 13 wins, four losses — including two in overtime — and three ties in their first 20 games. Turek was rewarded for his outstanding play with a new four-year contract worth a US$19 million. The goaltender became the highest paid player in Flames history.

After attending the Canadian Olympic team's training camp in September, Iginla also joined the Flames in excellent condition. He served notice that he and the Flames intended to shine this season.

Almost immediately afterwards, Calgary's fortunes nosedived. The Flames went winless between November 17 and December 3. Over the next two months, the Flames recorded only seven wins — even though Iginla counted 12 goals and

6 assists in November to earn honours as NHL player of the month. Turek was suddenly colder than the Arctic, but coach Gilbert continued to use him, leaving Vernon to stew on the bench in what would be his final NHL season.

Iginla still enjoyed some good news in December: he was named to Canada's Olympic team. Three months later, after losing to Sweden in the opening game, Canada rallied and advanced to the Olympic final against the U.S. Iginla scored two goals and added an assist as Canada beat the Americans 5-2. Thanks to Iginla's fine play, Canada won its first Olympic gold medal 50 years to the day after the Edmonton Mercury's gave Canada its last one. Iggy was now a household name across the country.

Iginla's dream season continued when he returned to the Flames for the resumption of the NHL regular season. Playing with more confidence than ever before, Iginla notched his 50th and 51st goals of the season in early April. He became the first Flame to score 50 goals since Gary Roberts way back in 1991-92.

"Yeah, baby!" shouted Peter Maher — for the first time in several seasons — up in the radio booth.

Iginla finished the campaign as the NHL's top scorer with 52 goals and 44 assists. No other NHLer scored 50 that season. He garnered the Art Ross Trophy for most points in the NHL, the Rocket Richard Trophy for most goals, and the Lester B. Pearson Award as the most valuable player as judged by players. He also finished as the runner-up to Jose Theodore for the Hart Trophy following a rare split decision. However, all Iginla's awards were bittersweet. He became one of the few players in the NHL's modern era to win the scoring title even though his team failed to qualify for the post-season.

However, the Flames were beginning to show signs of real progress. Iginla and his linemate Craig Conroy, and a young defence corps were maturing together as a team. Conroy had tallied 75 points in a breakout offensive a year after being considered a checker for several seasons. Calgary's playoff chances looked good for a change. They looked even better in October, when the Flames acquired centre Chris Drury, considered one of the best young offensive players in the game, and solid two-way centre Stephane Yelle for Derek Morris, forward Jeff Shantz, and speedy winger Dean McAmmond.

With their linemate McAmmond gone, both Iginla and Conroy started the 2002-03 season slowly. Calgary won only three games in the opening month of October and started November by losing six straight. By late November, the Flames had only five wins to show for the entire season. Newspaper reports speculated almost daily on when the coach would be fired.

In a surprise move, team president King joined the team during a five-game road trip. On December 3, as the Flames prepared to play their final game of the trip in Denver, King contacted Gilbert in his hotel room and told him that his tenure with the Flames was over. For the second time since

2000, the Flames were about to go through a mid-season coaching change.

There was just one problem. Calgary had no permanent replacement for Gilbert.

Chapter 8
A New Bench Boss

Two days before the Flames axed Gilbert, the San Jose Sharks had canned coach Darryl Sutter. Although the Sharks were mired near the bottom of the conference standings and riddled with injuries, the firing caught Sutter by surprise. He had never posted a losing record since he began his coaching career. But he took the heat for San Jose's slow start to the season. Rather than sulk or stew at home, Darryl took his wife Wendy to the annual National Finals Rodeo in Las Vegas, saying, "It was something I always wanted to do." The trip to Vegas was just Sutter's way of dealing with adversity — which he had faced many times before.

Sutter had been Chicago's 11th choice, 117th overall

from the Lethbridge Broncos of the Western League in the 1978 entry draft. According to his brother Rich, Darryl's low selection stemmed from a serious knee injury, which had not been treated properly. Upset with being drafted so late, Darryl had instead signed with a team in Japan, where he counted 41 points in only 20 games. "He was the Darryl Sittler of hockey in Japan," recalled his brother. After returning to North America and signing with Chicago, Sutter won the American Hockey League's rookie award in 1980. He then joined the Blackhawks on a permanent basis. In eight seasons in Chicago, he scored 40 goals once and at least 20 goals in five consecutive seasons. The Blackhawks twice advanced within one series of the Stanley Cup finals with Sutter as captain.

Most of the time, he played in constant pain because of numerous knee operations. It eventually hurt to watch him play, said Rich, because he was trying to do on one leg what most players do on two. After the 1986-87 season, Darryl reluctantly announced his retirement, at the age of 29. He immediately launched a new career as a coach in the Blackhawks organization. He guided the Indianapolis Ice to an International League title, then returned to Chicago as an assistant coach. In 1992, he helped the Blackhawks reach the Stanley Cup finals, for the first time in more than two decades. After Sutter took over as head coach the next year, Chicago became a perennial Stanley Cup contender. In 1995, Sutter suddenly quit.

He decided that his then two-year-old son Christopher, who was born with Down Syndrome (an ailment that affects motor skills and IQ) needed him more than his team did. "I didn't agonize over it," said Sutter. "It was reality, it was the right thing. I had put myself ahead of my family for 17 years. My responsibility is as a father, first and foremost."

After two years at home in Viking, Alberta where — thanks to a satellite dish — he watched more games than ever before, he resumed his coaching career behind the bench of the San Jose Sharks at the start of the 1997-98 season. He inherited a 62-point club, which had missed the playoffs in four of the previous six seasons, and transformed it into a Stanley Cup contender. Under Sutter, the Sharks made the playoffs in each full season that he served. He became only the second coach in NHL history, behind the New York Islanders' legendary Al Arbour, to improve his team's point total in five straight seasons. The results were even more impressive, because the Sharks faced many injuries and contract disputes. Darryl rarely had a full roster to work with.

So Sutter may have been surprised but he was not worried when he was dismissed by the Sharks. He figured he would get another job sooner or later. While Sutter was vacationing in Vegas, Calgary's president Ken King appointed the ever-loyal MacNeil as interim coach. MacNeil only expected to be behind the bench for one or two games. He focused on getting the team ready for the new coach. The veteran Flames executive wanted to make sure that Calgary stayed in the fight for the playoffs.

Meanwhile, speculation about who would become the permanent Flames coach abounded. One report had Jim Playfair, head coach of Calgary's farm team in St. John, New Brunswick, on the verge of being hired. Playfair said he would only take the job if he was guaranteed to keep it the following season. When the *Calgary Herald* reached Sutter by phone, he said he would be interested, but so far it didn't look like the Flames were. December dragged on and Calgary still did not have a new coach. King refused to discuss who was being considered for the job. Behind the scenes, he quietly began negotiations with Darryl Sutter.

Despite the rumours and the uncertainty, MacNeil kept the team on an even keel as they posted victories over Colorado, Vancouver, Nashville, and Minnesota, a team managed by former Calgary GM Risebrough. It was clear that players were enjoying the game again — and the team was enjoying one of its best months in recent memory. MacNeil's supposedly brief coaching gig lasted 11 games as he finished with a 4-5-2 record.

Finally, on December 28, 2002, the Flames named Darryl Sutter as the 13th coach in its franchise history. The Flames post was a good fit for Darryl, said Rich Sutter, because he looked forward to moving his family back to his home province. During his first news conference, Sutter vowed to give the team an identity that the players would try to live up to every day — a winner's identity. In January, he guided Calgary to six wins, seven losses, and a tie. The Flames' turnaround was not surprising. After all, they had improved — temporarily as it turned out — under a new coach before. The question was: How long would the good times last under Sutter? In February, Calgary won only two of 13 games.

Despite the slump, the new coach continued to get good reviews. However, as the NHL's March trading deadline approached, fans, reporters, and players started to wonder how Calgary would fare. Rumours of potential trades surfaced and Iginla quietly worried about his future. The former NHL scoring leader was now the club's highest paid player at $7 million per season. The Flames might consider dealing him for a few players to save money. As the deadline drew nearer, he became more and more nervous. He wanted to stay in Calgary and help finish the rebuilding job that had started with the trades involving Nieuwendyk (for Iginla himself), Fleury, Sutter, and others from the 1989 championship team.

The trading deadline came and the Flames kept Iginla. In fact, they dealt for a player who had helped him in the past — Dean McAmmond — and who hopefully would help Iginla re-kindle his offence of a year earlier. The Saddledome was buzzing the next day as Calgary prepared to play the Toronto Maple Leafs. The excitement stemmed from the arrival of former Flame Doug Gilmour, whom the Leafs had re-acquired at the deadline from Montreal for a draft pick. Gilmour was returning to one old team while playing against another former team. The other ex-Flame, McAmmond, had worked out with the Flames in the morning and was also looking forward to playing with his old Calgary teammates again.

As game time approached, though, word spread that all was not right with the McAmmond trade. The GM had unwittingly broken a rarely necessary rule in the collective bargaining agreement. Once a player was traded, he could not be traded back to his former team within 12 months of the original deal. Less than half a year had elapsed since McAmmond was traded to the Avalanche. The league later ruled that McAmmond would have to sit out the rest of this season.

Sadly, Gilmour also suffered misfortune. Early in the second period, Flames winger Dave Lowry, who had his back to the play, collided with the former Toronto captain in the neutral zone. Gilmour crawled to the bench with a severe knee injury that ended his season — and his career.

Fortunately, another trade that Calgary made did go through as planned. The Flames acquired Shean Donovan from the Pittsburgh Penguins for a couple of minor-leaguers. On the surface, the deal appeared to be a salary dump as the Flames unloaded two contracts in exchange for one. Donovan had counted only nine points in 52 games with the sad-sack Penguins. The Timmins, Ontario, native had started his NHL career under Sutter in San Jose in 1994-95.

Since he had played for Sutter before, Donovan's acquisition suggested that the coach was gaining greater influence within the Flames organization. However, the trade was questionable. Based on his career stats, the offensively challenged Flames could not expect Donovan to do much more than check. Before he left Pittsburgh, his career had apparently reached rock bottom. Fans could only hope that Sutter knew something about him that other coaches did not. After donning the Flames' uniform, Donovan again struggled to produce. However, his lone goal in a Calgary uniform proved to be the overtime game winner against Marty Turco, the league's top goaltender. Maybe Sutter had inside knowledge after all.

Although he wasn't scoring much, Donovan was helping the Flames win. After a terrible February, Calgary posted winning records in the final two months of the season, giving Sutter a respectable 19-8-8 record with the team. But for the first time in his NHL coaching or playing career, Darryl Sutter missed the playoffs.

At the end of the season, more changes loomed. Sutter received the added duties of general manager. Now, in addition to coaching the team, he would have to build the team. He would also draft, trade, and sign players, hire scouts, and oversee off-ice training schedules. As the Flames attempted to climb the proverbial mountain, almost every important decision would fall on Sutter's shoulders. Fans had to wonder, what did he know about managing a hockey organization?

Sutter's biggest challenge in the off-season was to sign

Chris Drury. Since his arrival the previous October from Colorado, reporters had speculated that Drury did not want to play in Calgary. Although he claimed that he liked Calgary, his usually glum facial expression suggested that he wanted to play elsewhere. As a result, the Drury deal threatened to become an albatross like the Gilmour trade of a decade earlier. After the strong finish to the regular-season, at least from the perspective of selling tickets, Calgary could not afford to have another key player hold out. May and June came and the Flames boss grew tired of what he viewed as an impasse. On July 3, 2003, Sutter traded Drury to the Buffalo Sabres in return for defenceman Rhett Warrener and forward Steve Reinprecht, whom the Sabres had acquired earlier in the day in a separate deal with Colorado.

Warrener didn't waste any time displaying his love for the Flames. On the day of the trade, the Shaunavon, Saskatchewan, native happened to be in Calgary for the annual Stampede, the exhibition that attracts a million visitors from around the world. He showed up for a news conference at the Saddledome on the Stampede grounds sporting a black cowboy hat and told reporters how much he was looking forward to playing in Calgary. In actual fact, he was just glad to be playing. A few months earlier, the defenceman had been involved in a bizarre incident. He was quarantined because he had been potentially exposed to the deadly Severe Acute Respiratory Syndrome (SARS), through his roommate's sister. Fortunately, Warrener showed no symptoms and doctors cleared him to re-join the club.

At the age of 27, Warrener became Calgary's oldest — and most experienced — defenceman. Drafted by Florida Panthers in the second round in 1996, he had achieved more than most of the players drafted ahead of him in the first round. Most of the 1996 first-rounders were not even in the NHL. After entering the league as a teenager, Warrener was already an eight-year veteran — and he had played in two Stanley Cup finals with Florida and the Buffalo Sabres.

Reinprecht was another example of a player who excelled after not being expected to do much. Perhaps because of his previous injuries, the scouts had overlooked the six-foot-one and 190-pound Edmonton native — even though he fit the NHL's prototype of a big, hard-working, and talented forward. Despite being a high scorer in junior, midget, and college, where he was also a four-time all-star with the vaunted University of Wisconsin Badgers, Reinprecht was not drafted. After being named as the Western Collegiate Hockey Association's player of the year and an all-American, he signed as a free agent in March of 2000 with the Los Angeles Kings. In the 2000-01 season, he finished fifth among rookie scorers with 15 goals and led all first-year players with five short-handed tallies. But he would stay with the Kings for only 59 games that season. Colorado insisted that he be included in the blockbuster deal that brought former Los Angeles all-star defenceman Rob Blake to the Avalanche on March 22, 2001. As a result, Reinprecht, like Fleury, became one of the few players to win the Stanley Cup as a rookie.

In his first major trade, Sutter had pulled off a sleeper. The deal worked financially and, more importantly, on the ice. Warrener and Reinprecht could step into Calgary's lineup immediately. Unlike previous deals, the Flames would not have to wait for future draft picks to develop. The future was now. In addition to acquiring players with talent and experience, Sutter had obtained players who knew how to win.

Meanwhile, two players acquired earlier — Yelle and Martin Gelinas — had also won Stanley Cups. In fact, Gelinas had reached the finals with three different teams. As a teenager, as part of the 1988 trade that sent Wayne Gretzky to Los Angeles, Gelinas won a Stanley Cup with the Edmonton Oilers. He also helped the Vancouver Canucks reach the 1993-94 finals, and his strong play enabled the upstart Carolina Panthers advance to the final in 2001-02.

Gelinas, Yelle, Reinprecht, and Warrener could serve as role models for the homegrown Flames who had little or no playoff experience. So could another player, who, just because of his position, was probably the most important Flame of all — Roman Turek. The goaltender had won a Cup title with Dallas in 1998-99 as a backup to Ed Belfour. He had also helped St. Louis reach the Stanley Cup semi-finals in 2000-01. But he had not performed well in Calgary since his hot start in 2001-02, just before he signed his big contract. The 2003-04 season offered Turek a chance to redeem himself.

Despite Turek in goal, Calgary opened the campaign

Oleg Saprykin, Calgary vs. Toronto, September 17, 2000.

with a humiliating 4-1 loss to Vancouver. Then, in the second game of the regular season, San Jose forward Alyn McAuley crashed into Turek, his knee colliding with the goalie's head. Turek was forced to leave the game, until doctors determined that he did not suffer a concussion. He soon returned to the lineup — but his comeback was short. A week later, only a minute and a half into the first period against Buffalo, he attempted to stop a shot by Ales Kotalik. Turek injured his knee and was again forced to the sidelines. This time, he would miss at least a month because of a sprained medial collateral ligament. Suddenly, the Flames had a major hole in goal.

The team's other goalie, Jamie McLennan, a career back-up, had spent the entire 2001-02 season in the minors because he could not crack the lineup of the parent Minnesota Wild. No other NHL team wanted him. Dany Sabourin, officially a rookie, was called up to take Turek's place on the roster. After three full seasons in the minors, he had no NHL experience. First-year minor pro Brent Krahn, a former Calgary Hitman drafted in the first-round in 2000, showed great potential, but was definitely not ready for the NHL. He was also recuperating from reconstructive knee surgery, which had kept him out of action almost two seasons.

With McLennan and Sabourin sharing the load, Calgary won only four games in October. In November, the losses continued. What a difference a year didn't make. The Flames were playing as poorly for Sutter as they had for Gilbert. On November 15, the Flames lost 2-1 in overtime to the Oilers in Edmonton — and Sutter came home unhappy.

The very next day, he traded a conditional second or third-round 2005 draft choice to his old team, the Sharks, for Miika Kiprusoff. "What do I like about him?" asked Sutter in response to a reporter's question. "He's an experienced NHL goaltender who's not 40 years old." Kiprusoff hardly looked like a saviour. Despite his coy comment, Sutter knew that "Kipper" could rise to a challenge. When Sharks starter

Evgeni Nabokov was injured in the first round of the playoffs against St. Louis, Kiprusoff had stepped in as a last-minute replacement. He stopped 39 shots as the Sharks beat the Blues 3-2. He became the first Finnish goaltender to win a Stanley Cup playoff game; he allowed only three goals in his first five NHL post-season contests.

Although he had posted a respectable 7-6 record in 2001-02, Kiprusoff played poorly in 2002-03 so fell to third-string status under new San Jose coach Ron Wilson. So far in 2003-04, Kipper had not played a single game with San Jose. If they had wanted to send him to the minors, the Sharks would have to put him on unrecallable waivers. Any other NHL team could pick him up without having to supply any players in return. Since he wasn't playing, and his previous season's record was shaky, his value on the trade market was low. By dealing him to the Flames for a draft choice, at least San Jose could get someone for him. And the Flames did not have to surrender a regular for someone who could best be described as an experiment.

Although Kiprusoff had not played that season in San Jose, he had practiced — almost every day — and learned under Sharks' goaltending coach Warren Strelow. Although rarely in the public eye, Strelow had helped turn San Jose into a goaltending mecca. In addition to Kiprusoff, he had tutored Nabokov, who was healthy again and had become one of the NHL's most consistent goaltenders. Strelow had also tutored former San Jose farmhand Johan Hedberg, who backstopped the Pittsburgh Penguins to an improbable berth in the Stanley Cup semi-finals in 2000-01. Two decades earlier, Strelow had even tutored Jim Craig as he helped the U.S. capture the 1980 Olympic gold medal.

Strelow also knew what it was to suffer. Instead of skates, he wore spiked shoes on the ice because he had lost a leg to diabetes. He was also on a waiting list for a kidney transplant. If Kiprusoff thought he had difficulties, he only had to look at his coach and friend for inspiration. On the evening before Kipper departed for Calgary, Strelow called him and gave him some final words of advice. He also warned members of San Jose's management that Kipper could come back to haunt them.

Sutter did not give Kipper a chance right away. The goalie had to watch as Calgary beat Toronto 3-2 in overtime on November 18 with McLennan in goal. On November 20, in his first game as a Flame, Kiprusoff stopped 22 of 23 shots as Calgary beat Montreal 2-1. It would be the first of many 2-1 victories — and first-star selections — as the Flames suddenly started reeling off wins.

In the first week of December, Kipper posted a 4-0-0 record and 1.00 goals against average, as the Flames beat his former Sharks team, Vancouver, Minnesota, and Pittsburgh. After a road loss to Minnesota, the good times continued for the rest of the month. Thanks to Kipper, who combined a butterfly style with the long-lost art of blazing across the crease, the Flames posted a 10-2-2 record in December.

Kipper, in goal for nine of those 10 victories, was named NHL player of the month. He also helped the Flames cope with a lack of scoring.

Iginla was struggling to reproduce his heroics of a year earlier, when he helped Canada to a gold medal at the Salt Lake City Winter Olympics. In his first 21 games, he had scored only five goals. Observers were starting to wonder whether the pressure of being named Calgary's captain was starting to get to him. At the age of 26, Iginla became the first black captain in the NHL. Craig Conroy had stepped aside in training camp, feeling Iginla was the best choice for the team.

As long as Kiprusoff was hot, it did not really matter whether Iginla was cold. Calgary kept winning and the early-season goaltending woes were all but forgotten. Turek was still out of the lineup with a knee injury. Contrary to the originally announced diagnosis of a month's recovery time, he had already been out two months. Calgary still remained in the top eight in the conference. A playoff berth, seemingly remote at the start of the season, was beginning to look more realistic. And then disaster struck the Flames again.

Kipper sprained his knee. The team announced that he would be out a month. With Turek still out of the lineup, McLennan, inherited the job by default. It was time for another unsung hero to pull the Flames through difficult times.

At the start of the season, Sutter had put McLennan

on waivers, attempting to see whether any other teams wanted to take him off Calgary's hands. There were no takers. For months, especially after Kiprusoff arrived, people had wondered how long "Noodles," as he was known to his teammates, would stick around. McLennan, a good-natured, happy-go-lucky type, was a big fan of the rock group KISS. He even painted pictures of Gene Simmons on his mask. But he knew he could kiss away his job if he didn't perform at this crucial time.

Noodles had joined Calgary in the summer of 2002 from the Minnesota Wild organization, in exchange for a lowly ninth-round draft choice. In his first season with Calgary, McLennan managed to record only two wins in the 22 games in which he appeared. Noodles vowed to do whatever necessary for his team. If he had to sit, he would sit. If he had to play — which he clearly wanted to do — he would play his best. Fans just wondered whether his best was good enough. Noodles, however, was yet another Flame who had faced adversity before. In May 1996, after spending a season in the minors, McLennan had come down with bacterial meningitis, a disease that attacks the lining of the brain. McLennan's kidneys shut down; he spent two weeks in hospital and lost 30 pounds. He spent the following season in the minors following his recovery, but the Blues signed him as a free agent. He posted a sparkling 16-8-2 record in 1997-98 and was awarded the Masterton Trophy. The Masterton goes annually to the player who exemplifies perseverance, sportsmanship, and dedication to hockey. And, McLennan would display those qualities again in 2003-04.

Although he was in the lineup when Kipper got hurt, McLennan was also quietly nursing a serious injury of his own. About two weeks earlier, in a game against Boston at the Saddledome, Noodles had taken a high, hard shot on the chest pad. Almost immediately, the goaltender staggered to the bench. After catching his breath, he returned to the Calgary net. Despite his injury, McLennan posted a shutout and was chosen as first star as Calgary blanked the Bruins 5-0.

Once he started playing in place of Kipper, it became obvious that McLennan was not in good health. At one point, reporters noticed that he could barely lift his catching glove. McLennan acknowledged that he was hurting, but he declined to give details on his injuries, attributing them to the wear and tear of playing. A few weeks later, McLennan revealed that he had been suffering from a broken sternum — an injury that might have kept others in bed. The sternum helps to protects the heart, lungs, and major blood vessels from damage. "Everything is tied into your chest," McLennan said weeks later. "The more you played, the more your muscles would spasm. I had a tough time holding my stick sometimes. The bottom line was I was going to play unless the doctors ruled it out."

Thanks to him, the Flames still stayed above .500 in the first two weeks of January as they counted three wins and a tie in their first six games of the new year. With McLennan playing in pain and Kiprusoff still another month away from returning, the Flames had no choice but to turn back to their former starter Turek.

In his first game back after missing 39 games, the Flames lost 3-2 to Dallas. But Turek earned a third-star selection as Calgary thumped Anaheim 5-1 and counted his 25th career shutout against Nashville. Still, Turek could not manage to win two games in a row. By then, Iginla was helping to keep the Flames in the playoff hunt.

Iggy recorded his first hat-trick on home ice February 3 and quietly moved into eighth place among NHL goal scorers. "Hopefully, this is the start of a run for me and my line," said Iginla. His comments would prove to be prophetic. Iginla did, indeed, start a marvelous run — around the same time that Kiprusoff returned from his injury. On February 10, after missing 19 games, Kipper launched the Flames on a four-game winning streak. It was their longest of the season.

Three straight losses followed. The long-awaited post-season berth was still in doubt. It was time again for Kiprusoff to work his magic — and he did not disappoint. On February 24, Calgary blanked Colorado 2-0. In the next 12 games, the Flames lost only three games. During that time, Sutter acknowledged that Calgary had put Turek on waivers. With the trading deadline approaching, the move was an obvious attempt to see whether any teams were interested in trading for him. But Turek would not leave the Flames.

Instead, in a move that saddened fans and players alike,

Noodles was traded at the deadline to the New York Rangers. The move spoiled a wonderful ride for the disappointed McLennan. He had looked forward to being part of Calgary's first playoff qualifier since 1995-96. McLennan's disappointment was Chris Simon's delight. As a result of the deal, he left the Rangers, who were already assured of missing the playoffs, to come to Calgary.

Simon, an Ojibway from Wawa, Ontario, was one of few First Nations players in the NHL. He had won a Stanley Cup with Colorado and helped Washington advance to the Cup finals. "Ron Wilson [then Washington's coach] was the first coach that I ever had that told me that I was a hockey player that was tough," said Simon. "I owe a lot of credit to him for giving me the confidence to become the kind of complete player that I'm trying to be." Simon's career had since stalled with weak teams in Chicago and the Big Apple. Although still known primarily as an enforcer, he also displayed an offensive touch. Sutter placed him on Calgary's top line with Iginla and Conroy.

Simon's intimidating presence gave Iginla and Conroy more room to work their offensive creativity. After acquiring Simon, the Flames tied Edmonton 1-1 and doubled Ottawa 4-2. Marcus Nilsson, acquired from Florida at the trading deadline, scored twice. After tying Nashville 4-4 in Tennessee, the Flames blanked St. Louis 3-0, dumped the Detroit Red Wings 4-1, and blanked the Columbus Blue Jackets 2-0.

Calgary stayed in sixth place, but a playoff spot was still

not guaranteed as the end of the regular season approached. On March 20, Calgary hosted Nashville in a return engagement but the Predators prevailed 3-1. With two seconds left to go in the game, after Nashville had scored an empty-net goal, Sutter sent out Krystof Oliwa, who immediately stirred things up. A brawl ensued. Even Kiprusoff dropped his gloves and fought Nashville netminder Tomas Vokoun. A day later, Sutter, who usually preached discipline, was suspended for two games for not controlling his team. Oliwa was tagged for three games by the NHL.

The next night, the Dallas Stars humiliated the Flames 4-0. This time, it was Simon who was suspended for two games. He was also fined $36,585.37 — for kneeing Dallas defenceman Sergei Zubov. It looked like the Flames were starting to unravel — at the worst possible time.

The Flames split road games in Phoenix, where they won 4-0, and San Jose, where they lost 3-2. On March 27, the Flames hosted the Los Angeles Kings, who they were battling for a playoff spot. The upstart Kings had stayed in the hunt all season long despite a plethora of injuries to several stars, including Adam Deadmarsh and Ziggy Palffy.

Simon returned from his suspension, looking to make amends for his mistake. In the second period, he committed another one. With the Flames trailing 1-0 early in the second period and on a power play, the puck came to Simon in the goal mouth — but he kicked it in and the goal was disallowed. But moments later, Simon re-directed a Jordan Leopold shot past L.A. goaltender Christian Huet, to create a 1-1 tie. After former Flame Jeff Cowan gave the Kings a 2-1 advantage, Conroy scored near the midway mark.

Both teams were scoreless in the third and went into overtime with a possible playoff spot on the line. Just a minute into the extra session, Calgary's Shean Donovan grabbed a loose puck near the Flames blueline and raced down right wing on a two-on-one with Conroy. Donovan looked over at Conroy, who wound up to one-time a pass. But with an L.A. defenceman in the middle and Huet leaning slightly, Donovan fired the puck over the goalie's glove as he stacked his pads. The goal gave Calgary a 3-2 win and effectively eliminated the Kings from the post-season.

"The whole way down, the puck was rolling a little bit and I was thinking pass and at the last minute I got a shot away," said Donovan. "I ended up getting it in, so it was nice." It was Donovan's first goal since February 1. As he had done on penalty shots earlier in the season, he slammed himself into the corner glass — and the crowd roared.

Iginla assisted on both of Calgary's regulation-time goals, earning his 500th and 501st career points. The milestone did not mean much to the Flames at this point — because a playoff spot was still not a done deal. The Flames could clinch a berth with a win over Phoenix at home.

That day, March 20, Flames co-owner Harley Hotchkiss, also the chairman of the NHL's board of governors, woke up at 5 a.m. in Toronto to fly to New York for league meetings.

The expiration of the collective bargaining agreement in September was a hot topic of discussion. He couldn't miss the meeting. Neither did he want to miss the Flames' potentially memorable night. When the meeting concluded, he raced out of the room, hopped a cab to the airport, and called his hotel's concierge. "You're not going to make it," she said. "You get me a boarding pass — and watch me," replied Hotchkiss. He even arrived at the Saddledome in time to have dinner. The crowd, cast in red shirts, was abuzz as the Flames and Coyotes, already eliminated from post-season contention, hit the ice.

Phoenix goaltender Brent Johnson was looking to redeem himself after recently joining the Coyotes in a trade. From the get-go, it was obvious that Johnson was having a strong night. But so was Kiprusoff, as he thwarted several early Phoenix chances. Before the first period ended, Regehr fired a pass across the goal mouth to Iginla, who fired the puck on net. Johnson foiled him. The puck was visible; sticks flailed at it and it went in. Although the goal was originally credited to Simon, officials later gave it to Iginla. "Simon came in and was whacking away and I initially thought he got it, " said Iginla. "But he told the ref he didn't and [officials] reviewed [the videotape]. I guess he gave it to me. It was very nice of him to be an honest guy. I didn't see it and, luckily, it went in."

It proved to be a critical goal — because nobody else could turn the red light on behind Johnson or Kiprusoff the rest of that night. "You can put it in the win column. Playoffs! Yeah, baby!" shouted Peter Maher over the radio and the Internet.

The best part, said the game's hero, Iginla, in the jubilant Calgary dressing room, was that the Flames did not have to rely on mathematics to get the post-season berth. "It feels good to win and not have to rely on another team," said Iginla. "This is the way we would have wanted it."

Iginla was just glad to be there. The Calgary captain recalled his anxiety of a year earlier when he thought he would be traded at the deadline. "I was really hoping I'd stay for a lot of reasons," said Iginla. "I really wanted to be here when we turned the first corner. I feel very fortunate that they've kept me here. It feels awesome. We've worked hard. We know this isn't the Stanley Cup or anything like that — but it's a huge step in growing as a team, getting better and, also, working towards winning one."

There was still one more bauble for Iginla to grab before the regular season ended. On the final Sunday, during a meaningless loss in Anaheim, he scored a goal to finish in a tie with Rick Nash of Columbus and Ilya Kovalchuk of Atlanta. All three finished with 41 markers to share the Rocket Richard Trophy. Meanwhile, Kiprusoff completed the regular season with a 1.69 goals against average — the best in the NHL's modern era.

Chapter 9
Back to the Stanley Cup Finals

The Flames drew the Vancouver Canucks in the first round of the 2003-04 Stanley Cup playoffs, evoking memories of their first-round triumph in 1989 — the last time they had advanced beyond the opening series. On paper, the third-place Canucks were the better team, but they were a team in turmoil. Late in the regular season, one of their stars, Todd Bertuzzi, had been suspended indefinitely for breaking the neck of Colorado's Steve Moore. Questions also surrounded the team's goaltending. Veteran netminder Dan Cloutier was looking to redeem himself following the Canucks' elimination at the hands of the Minnesota Wild a year earlier.

The Canucks took the first game 5-3 at GM Place. Calgary evened the series with a 2-1 win in game two — the first of many 2-1 games to come. When defenceman Sami Salo lost track of the puck after batting down a high shot in the Vancouver zone, rookie Mathew Lombardi whipped it home. Iggy scored the other goal.

Vancouver prevailed 2-1 in game three on Matt Cooke's winner. However, Vancouver suffered a major blow with 29 seconds left in the first period. After stopping an Oleg Saprykin shot, Cloutier lost his balance and fell backward, twisting his leg. He was out for the series. Johan Hedberg replaced Cloutier and performed admirably the rest of the night. Game four was no contest as the Flames blanked Vancouver 4-0 at the Saddledome.

Calgary also scored an important psychological victory. Temperamental Canucks coach Marc Crawford — the same coach who had kept Gretzky out of the shootout in the 1998 Winter Olympics at Nagano, Japan — decided to replace Hedberg with rookie Alex Auld. The Canucks had specifically acquired Hedberg in case something happened to Cloutier, but Crawford was abandoning him after only his second game as the starter. In game five, Iginla tipped home a shot with just under 15 minutes left in regulation to give the Flames yet another 2-1 win. They could clinch the series at the Saddledome two nights later.

Vancouver jumped out to an early, seemingly insurmountable 4-0 lead. The Flames rallied to tie the score 4-4 heading into overtime. Neither club could score for two extra periods. Early in the third extra session, as the Canucks were coming out of their zone, Vancouver captain Markus Naslund whacked Iginla's stick, knocking it out of his hands and behind him. As he tried to back up, Iginla tripped and fell on his bum as the Canucks raced up ice. The Calgary captain hustled back — without his stick — but Brendan Morrison scored to give the Canucks a 5-4 win and force a seventh and deciding game.

Again, the teams went to overtime with the score tied 2-2 after regulation. The extra session would not be nearly as long this time. Gelinas banged in Iginla's rebound 1:06 into extra time, giving the Flames their first series win since 1989. It also marked the second major series-winning goal for Gelinas. A couple of years earlier, he had netted the overtime winner when the Carolina Hurricanes eliminated the Toronto Maple Leafs in the Eastern Conference finals.

The Flames headed to Detroit for the second round. The Flames were clearly the underdogs against the Red Wings, who had finished first overall in the regular season. The Wings featured such stars as Steve Yzerman, Brendan Shanahan, former Flame Brett Hull, and yet another player the Flames had given up on — Robert Lang, who had been invited to training camp one season but wasn't signed.

Calgary shocked the Wings in game one at Joe Louis Arena as Nilsson converted Gelinas' pass from behind the net in overtime. The Flames skated to a 2-1 win. Yzerman stole

Martin Gelinas, Calgary vs. Toronto, January 13, 2004.

the show in the second game, scoring twice as the Red Wings romped to a 5-2 decision. The Detroit captain also accidentally clipped Flames defenceman Rhett Warrener near his right eye, sending him to hospital with blurred vision. But, back in Calgary, Iginla's second-period goal gave the Flames a 3-2 win in the third game — and a 2-1 series lead. Gelinas contributed two assists as all of the scoring was completed in the first 5:46 of the middle frame. The Wings played without veteran defenceman Chris Chelios. Saprykin, one of the smallest players on the ice, had sidelined him with a hit in the second game.

In game four, Gelinas and Villie Nieminen scored 18 seconds apart to help the Flames overcome a 2-0 deficit. Detroit still prevailed 4-2, evening the series again. With only three seconds left in the game, Nieminen rammed Detroit goaltender Curtis Joseph into his net and received a five-minute charging major and game misconduct. With his bone-headed actions, Nieminen, acquired from Chicago late in the regular season, broke up one of Calgary's most effective lines. He, Donovan, and Nilsson had all scored goals in three of the first four games.

The Flames didn't miss Nieminen in game five as Kiprusoff worked his goaltending magic. Conroy's goal with 3:53 left in the second period was the only goal that Calgary needed. The Flames skated to a 1-0 victory on the strength of Kiprusoff's 31 saves. "He made the saves. I don't know if he saw every one of them," Detroit coach Dave Lewis told reporters. "He made some big saves against a team with big-time goal scorers."

But the Wings suffered a major blow in the second period. Detroit's Mathieu Schneider fired a shot that ricocheted off Calgary defenceman Warrener's skate in front of Kiprusoff. It hit Yzerman squarely in the face as he stood to the left of the net. Yzerman, who doesn't wear a face shield, immediately sprawled to the ice, kicking his legs in pain. He was gone for the series with a left eye injury. "I think everybody on the bench was stunned," said Lewis.

On the day of game six in Calgary, the Red Wings' dressing room was like a funeral parlour as they faced the prospect of playing without their inspirational leader Yzerman. The Wings were also still without Chelios for the fourth straight contest. Kiprusoff and Joseph waged a goaltender's battle and there was no scoring in regulation time. Amazingly, with only 46.9 seconds left in the first overtime, Gelinas again notched the series winner as he banged in a loose puck from the side of the net. "They had more skill, but we worked extremely hard and it paid off," Gelinas said afterwards. "Everybody's been chipping in at different times and it's been fun."

The fun-loving Flames advanced to the Western Conference final against a team that could not help but evoke bad memories for Sutter and Kiprusoff — the San Jose Sharks. Sutter would have to prove that he was a better coach than the guy who replaced him, while Kiprusoff would have to outperform Nabokov. Donovan was also out to prove that San Jose had made a mistake by trading him. Grizzled veteran Dave Lowry was facing one of his old clubs, too, and former Flame Tim Hunter was now an assistant coach with San Jose, adding more flavour to an already interesting match up.

The Flames shocked the Sharks by taking the first two games in San Jose. But the Sharks retorted by winning the next two games in Calgary to even the series. Sutter replaced Kiprusoff in the second period of Calgary's 4-2 loss in game four. Kipper responded by shutting out the Sharks 3-0 back in

San Jose. The underdog Flames were now only one win away from qualifying for the Stanley Cup finals.

The Flames prepared for another close battle. Overtime — or "Marty Gelinas time" — would not be necessary this time, but the same ol' hero came through again. Gelinas notched his third series-winning goal as the Flames beat the Sharks 3-1 to the delight of the Saddledome faithful. Thanks to Kiprusoff, the Sharks scored just once in the final seven periods of the series.

After the game, Sutter and Iginla returned a call to Prime Minister Paul Martin. Martin wished the Flames luck as they returned to the final for the first time in 15 years. With no more Canadian teams left in the playoffs, the prime minister dubbed the Flames "Canada's team." Could the Flames carry the whole country on their hard-working shoulders?

Calgary's opponent in the final was the upstart Tampa Bay Lightning, which had finished first in the Eastern Conference. Tampa featured former Flames Martin St. Louis, who had already won the Art Ross Trophy for most points and was leading the playoff scorers. Cory Stillman, Chris Dingman, and several others who had once played in the Calgary organization were now playing for Tampa. At one point or another, several players in both clubs had been teammates with Calgary's farm club. Many had remained friends but, with the Stanley Cup at stake, all friendships were on hold until after the season.

In game one, Tampa's white-towel-waving fans were in

a frenzy after WWF wrestler Hulk Hogan's daughter sang the national anthem. Iginla gave them less reason to cheer when the Flames were shorthanded in the second period. The Calgary captain scooped up a loose puck, whipped by fallen defenceman Pavel Kubina and raced in alone on Lightning goaltender Nikolai Khabibulin. Iginla fired a wrist shot but Khabibulin —nicknamed the "Bulin Wall" — got his catching glove on it. The puck went straight up in the air as the out-stretched goalie fell to the ice. Iginla alertly stopped behind the left edge of the net, spraying up a huge wave of snow, but Kubina now circled wide on the right side. Iginla waited for the puck to fall and then tapped it into the net past the helpless Khabibulin. The shorthanded marker — Iginla's 11th goal of the post-season — stood up as the winner as Calgary won 4-1.

In game two, the Flames received an emotional lift as Lowry miraculously returned to the lineup after missing 43 games with an abdominal injury. At one point earlier in the season, Lowry had been helping the coaches on the bench. Reporters speculated that his playing career was over. The Lightning still struck back in the second game and pre-vailed. Tempers flared because Tampa players ran Kiprusoff a few times. "We got out-worked, out-hustled, and out-mus-cled. All kinds of outs. And now we are out of Tampa Bay," said Nieminen.

The Flames returned to the Saddledome and promptly blanked the Lightning 3-0. One goal was earned by Simon, who was starting to play like his old self after missing 10 games because of a knee injury. Donovan and Iginla got the other goals while Kiprusoff recorded his fifth playoff shutout. After his goal, Simon did his impression of Donovan and excitedly slammed into the corner glass. Donovan could not do his usual celebration dive because he was mauled by his teammates.

However, the Flames had little reason to celebrate in game four as early penalties cost them dearly. With the Lightning enjoying a five-on-three power play, Tampa forward Brad Richards, a native of Prince Edward Island, ripped a slapshot over Kiprusoff's catching glove just 2:48 into the game. The goal stood up as the winner. The Lightning remained undefeated for every game in which Richards had scored — in the playoffs or regular season. "This one hurts because it was a chance for us to go up 3-1," said Iginla. "It's a tough one to take. We didn't find a way to score."

It was also tough to take because of another careless late penalty by Nieminen. With a little more than four minutes remaining, he ran Lightning star Vincent Lecavalier from behind. "Definitely a penalty," said Sutter. "It's called a five-minute penalty because they react to the player going down. It's [really] a two-minute penalty." For the second time in the playoffs, league disciplinarian Colin Campbell suspended Nieminen.

The next day, Sutter reacted the same way Wayne Gretzky had done during the 2002 Olympics. There was a conspiracy against Canada's team, Gretzky claimed, after his team's disappointing start. During a press conference in Tampa Bay, Sutter commented on the penalty calling. "We have lost three players total to injuries ... there was a total of two minutes called. So fine, we know what we're up against," said Sutter. "We're the underdog...We're the little team that wasn't supposed to be here and a lot of people don't want us to be here and to make sure that we're not successful. We know that." Sutter was still upset that former Flame Stillman had not been suspended for a hit from behind to Nilsson's head in game one.

NHL vice-president Campbell defended his decision. "Nieminen used his forearm to deliver a forceful hit from behind to the head of his opponent," said the news release. "This hit was more severe than any of the other plays that were brought to our attention during the final. This was a hit that clearly crossed the line and was directed at the head. Even if Lecavalier is able to play in game five, this type of hit must be subject to supplemental discipline."

Even though he didn't change Campbell's mind, Sutter's ploy helped galvanize a city. Back in Calgary, Flames fever was reaching its highest pitch. Flames flags flew on vehicles throughout the city while some diehard fans painted their vehicles in Calgary's colours. More than 30,000 Flames' jerseys had been sold and retailers were having a hard time getting them from suppliers. One chain ordered all of its stores outside Calgary to send Flames' jerseys back to Cowtown as soon as possible. But even fans in Edmonton and Vancouver were snapping them up.

Business was also booming at bars on Calgary's 17th Avenue — which had become known as the Red Mile — and other pubs throughout the city. For the first time ever, the James Joyce Pub on Stephen Avenue Walk and The Joyce on Fourth had TVs installed.

The Flames needed all the help they could get from their enthusiastic fans — because injuries had taken an extreme toll on the team. Denis Gauthier had been out for weeks with a knee injury while Mathew Lombardi was out with concussion-like symptoms. Toni Lydman, Simon, and several others had missed extended periods of the post-season. Reinprecht had been out since the regular season because of shoulder surgery.

All the fan hoopla inspired the club in game five. The Flames came out with a much better effort in Tampa Bay and won 3-2 as Saprykin put in Iginla's rebound in overtime. The Calgary captain had lost his helmet in a scramble but still rifled a shot on goal. Iginla was practically unstoppable that game as he fired six shots, scored a goal, and set up the winner. The Flames just needed one more win to claim the Stanley Cup.

After the game, the Red Mile was again teeming with fans of all ages and backgrounds. The fans sensed that the Flames were on the verge of making history. Surely the Cup was coming to Calgary.

Could Iginla take them to the promised land the next game, enabling the Flames to parade with the Cup on home ice? Before the sixth game, NHL officials had carted the Stanley Cup to the Saddledome in a crate. They unpacked it as millions of fans across the country watched "Canada's hockey team" on *Hockey Night in Canada.*

Unfortunately for the Flames, the Lightning capitalized on their very first power play chance. With Jordan Leopold in the penalty box for interference, Richards got the puck at the goal line about 20 feet to the left of Kiprusoff. He launched a wrist shot that struck the goalie and caromed into the net at 4:17. No problem, fans figured. Richards' lucky streak had to end sometime.

Calgary's Chris Clark reassured fans by creating a 1-1 tie at 9:05 of the second period. He popped home a pass from Nieminen, who was back in the lineup after sitting out his one-game suspension. But the dreaded Richards tallied again. He corralled a rebound and fired it between Kiprusoff's legs at 10:52 of the middle period. It was his second power play goal of the game and 12th tally of the playoffs. Nilsson atoned for his error a few minutes later. He put in a pass from Saprykin to tie the game.

With about five minutes left in regulation time, slightly blurry TV replays showed that the puck crossed the Lightning goal line as Gelinas — looking for his fourth series winner — charged the net. Had he scored, the Cup waiting in the Saddledome would have been Calgary's. Play continued.

When the whistle finally blew, the on-ice officials, oblivious to the play, did not call for a video review. Neither did the Flames.

The score remained 2-2 after 60 minutes, but neither team could score in two overtime periods. Calgary fans settled in for a nail-biting wait. But in the opening seconds of the third overtime, Richards deflected Tim Taylor's point shot. The rebound came to former Flame St. Louis. He fired a snap shot that brushed Kiprusoff's blocker arm — and squeezed into the net. Tampa won 3-2 just 33 seconds into O.T. and evened the series.

Calgary's sure-thing Cup was suddenly no longer a sure thing. "We're all dead," St. Louis told ABC after the game. "I was too tired to celebrate. It's just nice to be out there and give ourselves a chance to bring it [the Cup] back." Iginla had been held to just two harmless shots in the game. As the series shifted to Tampa, the Flames were a banged-up club too. Donovan, hurt earlier in the season, could not play. Several others were either out of the lineup, or nursing aches and pains.

At the beginning of the seventh and final game, Calgary appeared to be overmatched. Scoring chances were few and far between as the Lightning stuck closely to Iginla. Tampa's Ruslan Fedotenko staked Tampa to a 1-0 lead in the first period and struck again in the second, giving the hosts a 2-0 edge after 40 minutes.

Just when things looked hopeless for the Flames, midway through the third, Conroy scored on a slapshot from just inside the blueline. For the rest of the period, the Flames blitzed the Tampa net. Khabibulin was unbeatable. The final buzzer sounded with Calgary pressing for the equalizer. The Lightning had claimed their first Stanley Cup in their 12-year history with a 3-2 win.

"In the end, we ran out of gas," concluded Sutter. Unofficial team spokesman Conroy added, "We had two chances, one at home, and we didn't get it done." As the Flames dejectedly shuffled off the ice, the hopes and dreams of their fans went with them.

Calgary's supporters did not stay dejected for long. Two days later, more than 20,000 of the loyal old and new Flames fans, some arriving at dawn, packed Calgary's Olympic Plaza. "This team has totally won the hearts of the city," said one fan, Cameron Shank, echoing the delighted crowd. "Some of these players no one knew... and every last one of them has become a hero."

As each of the old and new heroes was introduced to raucous cheers, some of the Flames players in white Stetsons had tears in their eyes. As they experienced the historic occasion, they praised the fans. "This is truly unbelievable," said Iginla, flashing his megawatt smile. "You guys helped to make this year and this run the time of our lives."

Thousands of people savoured the moment, bonded by a team that had made a miraculous run. Some of them could remember the club's good, and bad, times from years past.

Like the best Calgary teams that had gone before them, Iginla and his teammates had triumphed over incredible adversity. All of the fans at Olympic Plaza that day would remember the Flames of 2003-04 forever — and look forward to more exciting times in the future.

Acknowledgments

In the late 1980s and early 1990s, I covered the Calgary Flames for the *Calgary Herald*. In recent years, I have covered the team for Canadian Press and *Business Edge*. Over that time, I have observed some of the most memorable moments in Flames history. This book helps re-create those unforgettable moments. In addition to capturing Flames' history for posterity, my aim with this collection was to show how the Flames have contributed to some of the most important events and advancements in NHL history.

This book is dedicated to late Calgary Flames TV broadcaster Ed Whalen, a good friend, who loved the team more than anyone I ever met, but died before the Flames recovered from their seven-year funk.

Special thanks to Altitude's hockey editor Stephen Smith for asking me to write this tome and to Joan Dixon for her editing efforts. Thanks also to Kara Turner and Stephen Hutchings of Altitude Publishing for patiently waiting for my manuscript as the Flames completed their Stanley Cup drive in 2003-04.

This book was relatively easy to write because of the memorable work of some other writers and friends, including Gyle Konotopetz, who lent me his files, Eric Duhatschek,

Alan Maki, Tom Keyser, George Johnson, and Eric Francis. This book was also made easier because of help from some people in the Calgary Flames front office. Thanks to Peter Hanlon and Bernie Hargrave for arranging accreditation to games and practices at very busy times. Special thanks also to Peter Maher, Al MacNeil, and Ken King for granting my interview requests.

Last but not least, thank you for reading this story. This book took on extra meaning for me, because I wrote it while I was in the process of moving to Vancouver, my hometown, for business and personal reasons, after living in Calgary for many years. I moved to Calgary specifically to cover hockey and as a result developed many lasting friendships. This book will ensure that I never forget them.

Photo Credits

Cover: Jeff Vinnick/Hockey Hall of Fame; Paul Bereswill/ Hockey Hall of Fame: page 65; Dave Sandford/Hockey Hall of Fame: pages 97, 113.

About the Author

Monte Stewart has written about the National Hockey League since the 1980s. From 1987-93, he covered the Flames for the *Calgary Herald*. He continues to write about the team for various newspapers and magazines. His articles on hockey and other topics have appeared in such publications as *A Century of the National Hockey League, Hockey Today, The San Jose Mercury-News, Business Edge, Profit Magazine, The Daily Oil Bulletin, New Technology Magazine* and *Chicken Soup for the Preteen Soul*.

This is his second book. He is also the co-author of *Carry On: Reaching Beyond 100*, the autobiography of late Calgary centenarian Tom Spear. Stewart has also edited several books and articles and taught journalism, writing, and Internet-related courses at the Southern Alberta Institute of Technology, the University of Calgary, and other post-secondary institutions. After living in Calgary for almost two decades, Stewart returned to his hometown of Vancouver in the spring of 2004.

OTHER AMAZING STORIES

These titles are available wherever you buy books. If you have trouble finding the book you want, call the Altitude order desk at 1-800-957-6888, e-mail your request to: orderdesk@altitudepublishing.com or visit our Web site at www.amazingstories.ca

New AMAZING STORIES titles are published every month.